DEFINING WOMEN

... ON MATURE REFLECTION

Edited by Dianne Norton

Illustrated by Mig

Third Age Press

ACKNOWLEDGEMENTS

The opinions expressed in this book are not those of the editor or publisher but solely of the various authors.

I am deeply indebted to all the women who responded positively to my invitation to write something for *Defining Women*. Not only have they given freely of their time in writing and re-writing their pieces but they have also given generously of themselves in sharing their opinions, experiences and emotions – a gift more precious than time.

I am particularly grateful to Germaine Greer and Jan Etherington for allowing us to include writing previously published elsewhere and to the Rt Honourable Anne Widdicombe MP for taking up the 'Alphabiography' challenge.

I am also extremely grateful to the illustrator, Mig, whose enthusiasm for the project has resulted in inclusion of rather more of her wonderful, prescient and witty drawings than originally requested. I'm sure readers will agree that they contribute greatly to the style and quality of the book.

Thanks also to Gill Birchall for her careful proofreading of the text.

www.wwwow.info

. . . is a new website launched by Third Age Press *in conjunction with the publication of* DEFINING WOMEN.
It contains links to and details of organisations of interest to older women. We hope that this list will grow as more people and organisations discover the book and the website. Please feel free to contribute information.
Through the website readers can also express their opinions on the issues raised in DEFINING WOMEN.
WHY WWWOW?   WOW! Wonderful Worldly Wise Older Women?
or . . . ?

DEFINING WOMEN

... ON MATURE REFLECTION

Third Age Press

ISBN 1 898576 66 1
First edition

Third Age Press Ltd, 2007
Third Age Press, 6 Parkside Gardens
London SW19 5EY
Managing Editor Dianne Norton

Illustrations © by Mig
Cover design by Mig and Din

Layout design by Dianne Norton
Printed and bound in Great Britain
by IntypeLibra

CONTENTS

ORGANISATIONS OF INTEREST TO OLDER WOMEN

INTRODUCTION

Readers may feel this is a hodge podge of a book. One of the contributors did suggest, in the early stages, that the book needed a theme but I declined her advice. However, I have found that the pieces have, roughly, fallen into a number of sections – there are certainly connections and interesting parallels between many of them. My intention was to let women write about anything that was on their minds in the hope that it would light a spark in other minds as well as generate animated conversations.

Older women are, after all, as diverse a group of individuals as you'll come across anywhere and I hope that the variety in this book reflects that. The phrase – 'The Elderly' – so often used in the media (and not uncommonly coupled with the word 'burden' – a label we seem to share with 'taxes') – is a terrible denigration of the rich complexity of older women (and men, of course). It is said that, if anything, we become more like ourselves as we grow older and that certainly doesn't mean more like each other. We are not in any way an homogenous mass and this book demonstrates that important truth.

Doris Bancroft, in an introduction to a Study Day on Older Women in Feature Films (see pages 119 - 126), expresses this very well. *We* (older women) *are a growing proportion of the population; we are active in the arts, the professions, politics and at many levels of employment; we form an army of volunteers and charity workers; we are frequently unpaid care-workers; we are peace campaigners and activists in many causes; we make friendships and relationships, have fun, adventures and sometimes tragedies; we have pasts, presents and futures; we are not set in aspic (or tucked away in lavender), we are still growing and developing as people; and we are a force to be reckoned with in society. After all, the most powerful person in the country is probably an 80 year-old woman living just across the river at Buckingham Palace.*

The way we perceive ourselves is important to the way others perceive us. If we succumb to stereotypes then those stereotypes will be re-inforced. We've probably all come across old people who insist on proclaiming at every opportunity 'I'm 88, you know', as if the simple accomplishment of having lived so long is itself a source of pride or perhaps, sadly, their only badge of honour. If we can perceive ourselves as something other than an old person, as all the authors in this book obviously do, then others will see us as something other than just an older woman.

Given that, you may feel it is perverse of me to deny you the opportunity of knowing more about the women who have contributed to this book. With the exception of our three 'celebrity' contributors, the authors are women whose paths have crossed mine during 20 years of work with Age Concern England and the University of the Third Age, plus a smattering of friends and neighbours. I have decided not to include 'profiles' of the authors because I want their writing to stand on its own without the reader having any preconceptions about the writers other than what their writing tells you (which in some cases is quite a lot).

The idea for this book began to grow after Jessie Coning and Maggie Guillon sent me collections of their own, and while I did not feel that either of them would make a book in itself, I very much liked some of their work and thought it would fit into an anthology (as it has).

I had also read and been impressed by two anthologies edited by the late Canadian author, Carole Shields, *Dropped Threads* (1 & 2) written by women of all ages, mostly writers and academics.

While *Defining Women* may be a book that you read and hopefully enjoy, I hope it will also be one that will set your mind to work.

ETCETERAS

Most of the pieces are followed by an *Etcetera* (from a number of different sources) – sometimes completely random thoughts inspired by the writing; sometimes specific questions or comments to trigger thought and/or discussion; sometime practical information. You may think these are overly pedantic or even patronising (if so, I suggest you don't read them). Part of my reason for including the *etceteras* is because I hope the book will be used as a tool to kick start discussions in women's groups and thought the questions or provocative statements might be helpful. In addition, while editing the pieces, I invariably found my mind stimulated or littered with questions arising from what I'd read and couldn't resist the urge to share them.

It is my sincere hope that *Defining Women* will inspire readers to think about issues that are important to them. Who knows, some such musings may well constitute *Defining Women Part II*.

I have to admit that I was disconcerted when, in my search for organisations relevant to older women, I typed 'older women' into Google and was overwhelmed with pornographic references so I hope that by linking the book with a new website **www.wwwow.info** we will not only be centralizing a lot of useful information but will also provide readers with an opportunity to communicate the thoughts raised by the book.

I see the publication of *Defining Women* not as the end of a lot of hard but pleasurable work but as a beginning . . .

Dianne Norton

You are never too old to be what you might have been
George Eliot (Mary Ann Evans), novelist (1819-1880)

TWO BLESSINGS: HOME AND AWAY

Miriam Hodgson

At sixty-six, always introspective, I have decided to look back at the steps I have taken to reach the person I am now. I have gone on a journey from intense doubt and poor self-image to a woman more or less contented with who she is, except sometimes . . . I grew up at a time when anti-Semitism was muted by the Holocaust, I am now living at a time when anti-Muslim feeling is regrettably gaining strength. What I am now echoes my embrace of three cultures – German, Jewish and English. What brought my journey to its goal of contentment is the knowledge that two blessings strengthened my weaknesses. Let me take you to the beginning of my journey.

HOME
Friday night, Cambridge. Dr Erwin Rosenthal, my short but muscular father has exchanged his corduroy jacket and flannels for his Sabbath finery. He is wearing a grey poplin shirt and silk tie, with a grey suit, his shoes are immaculately polished as always. We sit at the Biedermeier flaming-birchwood dining table. The light of the white candles in the plain silver candlesticks (the work of his childhood friend,who emigrated from Germany to Israel where he taught at the Bezalel art school) creates a glittery glow from my father's silver threaded skull cap,

crocheted by my mother. There is the smell of fresh bread, as the poppyseed twists, the ritual chollah, baked by Maskells, the local baker, rests under the silk cloth, embroidered with a silver Star of David. In my early childhood the chased silver goblet was filled with cider, later, when finances were easier, with a favourite German Hock. The table setting is the white Rosenthal plates, the Greatgrandmother's German silver cutlery (later replaced by Georg Jensen stainless steel), and my mother's favourite mats of the Cluny tapestries. All these items were only used to welcome Queen Sabbath and make it different from the rest of the week.

My elegant mother wears a dress of soft crepe wool with ornate enamelled earrings and necklace. She has lit the candles, which distinguishes the Sabbath from the week – light after dark. She is waiting to bring in the fish dish with the butter and egg sauce.

NOW COMES THE BLESSING
The smell of Old Spice after-shave and Johnson's Baby Powder, the touch of my father's hands, so gentle and loving, so light and comforting on my head, as he recites the prayer to God to make me like Sarah, Rachel, Leah and Rebecca, the first matriarchs of Israel. He also asks God to

Miriam Hodgson

11

protect me in the coming week. I am given a piece of the blessed bread, sprinkled with salt from a tiny silver spoon, carefully measured by my perfectionist scholar father. My mother and brother Thomas, too, are blessed and share the bread.

Little changed in this ritual for more than fifty years. I left home, eventually got married and brought Elinor, my daughter, to receive Grandpa's blessing. That blessing has given me strength and still does, even though my father died 13 years ago. I can still smell the Old Spice, feel the gentle fingers on my hair and the transmission of my father's love and protection as well as God's.

The first Blessing of my life is and was my father. He gave me life and preserved it.

Now in 2005, sixty years since the liberation of Auschwitz, I am reminded of what I have always taken for granted. It was my father's foresight that allowed me to be born and to survive. When I forced myself to watch Lawrence Rees's BBC2 series *Auschwitz* and saw film of three-year-olds sent off to the camp in 1941, all I could think was I could have been one of those little girls, smiling, holding my mother's hand . . .

In Berlin in 1933, Hitler's laws forced my father, as a Jewish academic, out of the university and the libraries. The thousand-year-old Jewish community was threatened. Father had just got engaged to Elisabeth Marx, the daughter of Dr Hugo Marx, one of the first forensic scientists and a distant cousin of Karl Marx. Hugo Marx had died in 1920 after contracting TB while working as a doctor in the 1914-18 war. My father saw the writing on the wall and decided to emigrate to England with my mother. He was encouraged by his future mother-in-law, but they could never persuade her to join them because she had her senile mother to care for. My mother never discovered what had happened to them after the Russians captured Berlin. Several years after the fall of Berlin the Red Cross forwarded to her her mother's last letter saying that she and grandmother were in hiding with Lutheran nuns and the Russians were coming.

This was so traumatic she did not tell me about it until just before she died eight years ago – a state of unknowing that may well have accounted for her bouts of depression in her last years.

My father managed to get all his living relatives, except for his beloved youngest sister who died in a concentration camp, out of Germany. He also got out those of my mother's family willing to come to England.

My father arrived in London in April 1933, my mother in June, and in July they were married. For their honeymoon they chose an inexpensive boarding house in Westcliffe on Sea . . . 'Sorry, we only take Jews,' they were told. Nothing could have reassured them more that England would be their safe haven.

'Britain has shown more fair play to the Jew than any other country in the world.' Words spoken by the headmaster of Avigdor High School evacuated to Shefford in North Bedfordshire in August 1945 to thank the village for their hospitality.

(Quoted in Jonathan Freedland, *Jacob's Gift*, 2005)

Thanks to recommendations and his academic qualifications, my father was appointed to a part-time lectureship in Hebrew at University College, London. His academic life in England had begun. He went on to teach Old Testament Hebrew at Manchester University, and when war broke out he was called up. He was chosen to re-educate German prisoners of war in the ways of democracy for PID, (the Political Intelligence Department of the Foreign Office), in Egypt and England. He also lectured on philosophy and politics for the Workers' Educational Association. In 1949 a lectureship at Cambridge University allowed him to return to his real academic love. He had begun his edition of Averroes' commentary on Plato's *Republic* in Berlin twenty years earlier. At Cambridge he completed it and went on to write more books on Islam as a political philosophy in medieval times and the present. He admired Islam and Muslims greatly and found nothing incompatible in this with being an ardent Zionist. I am glad he was spared today's situation. In September 2004, the centenary of his birth, I was delighted to find his books in the Al Furqu'an Foundation, an Islamic study centre in Wimbledon.

If I have to define the essence of my father, it was his passionate tolerance, his true egalitarianism that made him a socialist. He never had much money and spent so little on himself but there were always books and records, tickets for concerts, visits to art galleries and weekly flowers for my mother, whose increasing invalidism made this most impatient of men into a perfect carer. He was a political philosopher, a political idealist, who in a perfect age would have wanted a theocracy. The age of Enlightenment was probably his favourite period of European history, the birth of toleration. He was not an orthodox Jew but the German Liberal equivalent of Jewish, English Reform, and every day of his life he said his prayers. In Cambridge, where there was no rabbi, it fell to my father to officiate at weddings and funerals. He was a natural preacher as his wonderful morale-boosting letters all my life showed. He cared for the underdog, be it adult or

child. He had the German love of the arts, which he shared with my mother. Perfectionism was not only in his scholarship but also, when he became housekeeper to my invalid mother, he applied the same rigorous standards to this new career, however irksome he found it, however frustrated he was to see it sapping his energy, leaving no room for scholarship. He was outspoken, delivered the truth when it had to be given. Robert Westall, the great children's writer, told me, when he saw the photo of my father included in *The Independent*'s obituary, that if he ever met God he thought he would look like my father.

AWAY

It was while teaching at University College London, that a colleague introduced him to the second blessing that I have taken through life, Ruth and Rosemary Spooner.

Sunday lunch, Oxford, I am sitting at a round oak dining table, placed under a strikingly real reproduction, even to its triptych form, of Van Eyck's 'Adoration of the Lamb' in Ghent cathedral. On the table are old Rockingham plates, repaired with rivets, Georgian silver, a bottle of Heinz salad cream, a salad of lettuce leaves, whole tomato and sliced cucumber, a jug of water. Sitting with me are a Yorkshire miner on a scholarship to Ruskin College, the master of an Oxford college and his wife, and the cousins Rosemary and Ruth Spooner, the hostesses. At the far end of the room is the Bechstein on which, after tea to which many more visitors would come, Ruth would give a recital

The Spooners represented for me, a literary child, Trollope and Jane Austen come to life. Rosemary's three sisters were married to, respectively, Dean Inge,

Campbell-Dodgson, Keeper of the Prints and Drawings at the British Museum, and the socialist Admiral Murray, whose daughter became the first principal of New Hall, Cambridge. The Spooners' house in North Oxford epitomised Oxford history. It was built after fellows of colleges were allowed to marry in 1860. Rosemary and Ruth's fathers were brothers. They married two Goodwin sisters. Ruth's father, the elder, was a fellow of Magdalen and on his marriage had to resign his fellowship but obtained a college living and ended his clerical life as a Canon of Canterbury. Rosemary's father married after 1860 and could remain a Fellow of New College and eventually became Warden. (The current Oxford English Dictionary no longer attributes the 'Spoonerism' to him and Rosemary supported that view and reported that on the publication of the first Oxford Dictionary Warden Spooner said, 'I understand that I have gained some notoriety'.)

These two cousins were in their late sixties, early seventies in my time at Oxford in 1956-60. Rosemary with her auburn gold hair, which never greyed, was handsome and imposing. Her eyes behind the gold spectacles could glint fiercely as well as greet warmly. She had been chairman of the Radcliffe Hospital Board, a Labour city councillor, educated at the Society for Home Students, which was to become my college, St Anne's. Ruth, by contrast, was gentle, loving, tiny, with snowdrop-white hair and a face like a medieval English alabaster. She was intensely musical and a gifted pianist who gave recitals in psychiatric hospitals and prisons.

The Spooners have remained for me the cynosure, the best of my Oxford years. They gave me my love of the English landscape which came to fruition after I had married my equally English husband. If my parents gave me German and Jewish culture and Jewish ethical values, the Spooners epitomised for me what is finest about the best of England and the English Christian socialist values. Perhaps the two are not so very different? Service to God and to fellow humans was their watchword. There was no money to speak of but there was a beauty in the simplicity of their life, its generosity to others, its punctuation by beauty in the form of a perfect Englishwoman's garden, Rosemary's work, and music, epitomised by Ruth. They were full of generosity and loving kindness that the first world war had prevented them from lavishing on husbands and children. They reinforced my parents' values. I basked in so many of their loves – Italy and the Lake District where they took bicycling holidays. I loved their fair-mindedness, their courtesy, their total lack of vulgarity.

We are now obsessed by lifestyle and how to achieve it, if only I could distil the essence of Spooner to permeate the pages of magazines and papers and our TV screens. Their watchword which sat happily with their fine aesthetic sense was ' Furnish your minds and not your houses.' Their Christianity embraced the stranger, the Jew, without one moment's thought that they had to convert them.

I think subconsciously I admired them, too, because they were at totally at ease with themselves, the carapace of the English Liberal perhaps? This was an ideal I was to strive for although I was content to keep my Germanness in my make-up. I saw my Germanness Anglicised as in the Schlegels in E M Forster's *Howard's End*, but without what I found, on re-reading the novel last year, the patronising attitude to Leonard Bast.

In Cambridge my parents entertained Jewish students every Saturday, in Oxford the Spooners entertained Ruskin students, graduate students, and undergraduates to tea on Sundays, a tea that included scones, made by Rosemary with the milk that was put to sour in the basement pantry. Tea was followed by a piano recital from Ruth. Phaidon art books lay on tables welcoming attention. Sunday supper followed Ruth going to a service at the university church, St Mary's, and Rosemary to St Giles, both on their bicycles. This was the only meal of the day taken without guests unless someone was staying. In the groundfloor flat of their house lived a Ruskin student and his wife, rent free. The Spooners' goodness was palpable in its practicality. They showed their concern for others, their dedication and sense of service and to this end they gave their considerable gifts. They were balanced in their opinions, unprejudiced. They honoured the individual and his beliefs and conscience. Like the Jewish tradition their door was open to everyone in need, regardless of colour, class or creed.

Perhaps it was the mixture of Jewish and Spooner values that, in my last term at Oxford, led me to consider training to become a hospital almoner (now a medical social worker). But the head almoner at the Radcliffe ended those dreams when, after assessing me and my wishes carefully, she decided that, even with professional training, I would take cases too much to heart and allow my judgment to be clouded. I went into publishing instead and, fortunately, taking my authors and their characters to heart did not risk such potentially dangerous results.

If I try to define what ideals I have attempted to follow and whose examples have inspired me, my first ideal is the Jewish sense of duty, to give something to others, to 'repair the world' to quote Jonathan Freedland again:[The Jews] 'believe they have a specific contribution to make, the task for which they were 'chosen.'. It is to spread the wisdom of the Torah, an ethical guide to living. The mission statement is summarized in the two words of the core obligation of *tikkun olam*, 'repairing the world'.

The second ideal is to live in a way that is my thank-you to England, the country that not only allowed my existence but also gave me the best education and opportunities for a career, and led me, finally, to my third blessing, my husband and daughter.

My father and the Spooners are the two blessings that helped me try to achieve these aims even on a rather private stage and without what some would consider the necessary accompaniment of religious observance. Both set me examples of the 'good life' in its deepest sense. I became a children's book editor and always looked for the highest quality, and for books that stretched and comforted, that made children empathetic to children from other times, other countries, other living conditions. They often showed children who had to fight adversity and problems not of their making, problems caused by their families, politics or history. They had to show, too, that hope was never entirely absent even in darkest times. The patience my teacher father showed to me, I tried always to show to my authors in helping them but never forcing them to shape their stories and characters. I tried to guide them with the least intervention to let their stories 'repair' the world of the child.

So I have lived my whole life under two blessings – one consciously given, the other set by example. I modelled my Englishness on the Spooners. I tried to achieve their unassuming, quiet serenity. I work beyond retirement, a reminder of their devoted service to so many causes well into their eighties. In a far more class- ridden age than now, they judged by behaviour. They gave me my overpowering love of England's literature, history and land-scape. They were true socialists with no nod to the class system .

My father's understated Jewish faith sustained him through a long and often difficult life. I inherited that faith even though it has been much modified to survive without observance of rituals. Did I lose my Jewishness? To my embarrass-ment the news that I am Jewish is often greeted with 'I would never have thought so.' This is meant as a compliment which, in English style, I deflect, I hope without giving offence. I am Jewish. How can any Jew after the Holocaust deny their Jewishness or ever stop thanking God for their personal survival? I feel guilt easily but my marriage to an Anglican has never felt like a betrayal of my Jewishness. My parents' extraordinary tolerance helped me with their loving welcome of Julian. I know there is a view that the high numbers of Jews marrying out – it increases yearly – is Hitler's ultimate victory. But I do not think Jewishness is so easily left behind, the ethics of Judaism go with all Jews. The virtues I learned from my father I still strive to observe even if the religious rituals have gone. Like him, I still believe in the hope that one can leave the world a better place.

How do I cope without the rituals? I do miss the Passover service, and on the eve of the Jewish new year I still dip a slice of apple in honey to signify the hope for sweetness in the coming year. When Elinor was a child we had Chanukah, the festival of lights, as well as Christmas. I still avoid pork because Jews died for the freedom not to eat it.

The rituals Julian and I created for Elinor were secular, we decided she should be allowed to choose her religion and at the age of thirty she was baptised.

She acquired her Christian knowledge at school. I am perhaps most moved by Chris-tian-influenced painting – Poussin's 'The Seven Sacraments' at the Scottish National Gallery in their special room which, though unconsecrated, is as holy as any church. I am most moved by Christian-inspired music in the form of Bach cantatas and his Passions and the B Minor Mass. One of our rituals is to listen to the Richter recordings of the cantatas on their due dates throughout the year. I regard these works of art as expressions of the love of a God who has inspired man to be his finest and most humane.

We all shared my father's Seders, that celebration of freedom. Elinor was taught about Jewish festivals and I read her Bible stories. But though there is no Friday night, I do light candles and find them holy. I hope I have passed on to Elinor what my Jewish father had given me. I brought to my marriage the Jewish experience that survived generations of persecution, the knowledge that marriage and the family is the most important and precious ingredi-ent of private life.

Today there is a ceremony for becoming a British citizen. My father's generation of German refugees seeking citizenship, if lucky, had a Rosemary and Ruth Spooner in their life to learn what it was to be Brit-ish, and to love them was to love their county. If only every asylum seeker and new citizen had the blessing of a couple like the Spooners in their lives. Greater racial harmony, born of mutual respect and acknowledgement of shared ethical ideals would be the result.

Miriam Hodgson sadly died in November 2005. When asked to contribute to this book she had welcomed the opportunity to reflect on her life and a portion of 'Two Blessings' was read at her memorial service.

etcetera

We are used to considering the impact that nature and nurture within the family have on the development of our character and the identity that we take for ourselves but perhaps, unlike Miriam, we don't pay as much attention to what influences people outside the family have on making us who we are.

No matter what our upbringing, ritual or tradition – whether religious, cultural or personal and social – will have 'glued' various occasions into our memories. Quite often these will take the form of a collage rather than a specific memory of one occasion. Such events are useful triggers for reminiscence.

RUSKIN COLLEGE

Just as it did in Miriam's Oxford of the 1960s, Ruskin College still provides educational opportunities for adults with few or no qualifications. See page 141 for details.

CHARACTER

Audrey Cloet

Is character inborn, or is it shaped by the experiences which befall us?

I've often wondered why I became one of life's fighters, why other people think of me as a bit of a rebel and why it doesn't seem to disappear as I grow older. The vision of myself as an increasingly benign and wise old lady now seems unlikely.

When did it start? I have clear memories of being outrageous at secondary school, the class comedian and the one who would always rise to a dare. Looking back, there were reasons – being a council house kid at a posh girls' school, being a year younger than everyone else in the class and being teased for being small. Was it then that I learnt to fight back? My cousin, nearly two years older and my childhood playmate, insists that from the first I was a scallywag, always the instigator of games that got us into trouble. Of course I don't believe him! However, I do remember persuading the sweet little girl next door to pour buckets of water down a bank in her garden to make a mud slide, getting spectacularly filthy and being walloped by my mother. That was before I even went to school, so perhaps my cousin is right.

So back to the beginning – we mothers know that even in the maternity ward babies are not alike. Earlier still – nurses in premature baby units see differences in behaviour. My own little miracle pound-and a-halfer was nicknamed 'peanut' (or 'peenut'!) for her persistence in turning round in the incubator. She has more scope for her bounding energy nowadays, but she still has that quality of hanging in there even though the going is tough. So is character truly inbuilt and not acquired?

I think I wasn't the easiest (ie. pudding-like) child to bring up and my mother used to say 'our Audrey is highly strung'. What on earth did that mean? I know that one day when a gypsy came to the door, mother said she thought I had St Vitus's dance! The wise-woman gypsy recommended a daily dose of the dried leaves of mistletoe – enough to cover a silver threepenny bit. I had this for ages; one day I'll look it up in Culpepper to see if it really is a herbal remedy.

Obviously not a permanent cure, for fast forward through an outwardly conventional life of teaching, marriage and children there are markers to indicate the possibility of growing old disgracefully. 'Oh why can't you be like Mrs Wickison!' from an exasperated daughter – very wounding, as I tried so hard to be the pink gingham pinny kind of mother. It became a family saying, a rueful admission that I fell short of perfection in the domestic role. Not, you understand, in the really important arts of making an angel costume for the nativity play – overnight because the little darling forgot to tell you – or creating the most amazing birthday cakes.

What is character? Is it a kind of core determined by the genes, which sets the pattern for responding to the experiences that life throws your way? To say that someone has 'acted out of character' is to assume the stability of this core and to claim that only some extraordinary event would have rocked it – and consequently this merits forgiveness. The dictionary definition as 'the combination of traits and qualities distinguishing the individual nature of a person or thing' isn't helpful – that 'individual nature' is what most of us would think of as character!

There are those who maintain that nurture is more influential than nature in shaping character, but I am not convinced. It affects behaviour, since experience teaches us to modify our natural responses, and a favourable, stimulating environment might encourage development of our talents, but that is not the 'essential me'. We all know that people react differently to seemingly similar events – that some fall apart in adversity, whilst others survive and even use the experience positively.

It's that 'individual nature' again – it seems that, like a stick of seaside rock, we have our character stamped all the way through us.

etcetera

Is there a difference to having a character and being one? It seems that when someone remarks to the mother of a lively child 'My, my, little Daisy IS a character, isn't she?' it's not really a compliment.

Do many of us reveal our true character most of the time? We've all been to funerals of people we thought we knew well only to find that, as the various eulogies were given, we begin to wonder whether this is the same person we did know. Of course, people rarely 'speak ill of the dead' but isn't it usually the case that we show different aspects of our character to people we meet in different situations and there are very few people, if any, in our lives, who see the whole us? Maybe that suggests that nurture is more important than nature – as we adapt our inner character to fit the various aspects of our lives. Or does it mean that that inner core is what keeps us 'together' through the twists and turns of experience?

In actor and broadcaster Stephen Fry's documentary on living with bipolar disorder (or manic depression), one of the most interesting revelations was that he, and all but one of the people he interviewed said, if there was a button they could push to make their bipolarity go away for ever, they would not push it. They see it as part of who they are despite the frightening draw backs. What does that tell us about 'character'?

DEFINING WOMEN

WILL THE REAL JOYCE SMITH PLEASE STAND UP . . .

Joyce Smith

On my 63rd birthday, in 1991, while walking in West Scotland, I tumbled off the mountain and fell some 200 feet, bouncing off rocks and various bits of vegetation as I went but, miraculously, ended up with no broken bones, a cut that needed stitching and quite a few bruises. The medics in the hospital (where I was transported my helicopter) put my good fortune down to the facts that I was a runner (an activity that had strengthened my bones) and that I relaxed as I fell – I thought to myself 'Oh, so this is how it's going to end' – I was convinced that I was going to die and there was no point trying to stop myself.

The local press picked up on the story of the tumbling 'elderly' 63-year-old and the 200 feet became 600 – and it somehow ended up on Capital Radio as 'Granny plunges 600 feet and defies death!'. According to the Surrey Comet I was a 'pensioner' who had 'cheated death miraculously' and the Daily Express trumpeted 'Peak fall gran lives' which prompted a letter in response headed 'Gran Canyon' wondering why people tempt fate in such fashions.

The distortions that annoyed me most were that I was neither a pensioner nor a grandmother but because I was over 60, the media had made assumptions about me that were just not true. They weren't interested in the fact that I was and had been for many years a primary school teacher, had an OU degree in psychology and was a marathon runner – and that's how I identify myself, as a runner. People who knew me from my teaching still remember me as a runner. I like to think that when I die it will be the running that comes out at the funeral.

I started running at 53 when a friend who needed to lose weight convinced me to join her on Wimbledon Common and then gave up, exhausted, after 10 minutes. I had just got into a rhythm and was angry at having to stop and take her home. But even that short jog had made me realise that I liked running.

Shortly before this incident I'd consulted a marriage guidance counsellor about the boredom I felt with my husband and his disinterest in getting out and doing anything – we never did anything together. We were getting on each others nerves and quarrelling. She suggested I needed to get out and do something for myself. When I complained that he just sat there watching television she suggested I watch it with him. I tried but as he mostly watched sport my incessant questions about why they were doing what they were doing got on his nerves and he said 'for heaven sakes, go in a another room and do something else'. Running rescued me from the boredom but, at least for the next few years, didn't do much for my marriage as I got so enthusiastic that I was always out training or running races. He complained about getting his Sunday dinner on time but thought that after I'd done a good marathon time I'd feel I'd attained my goal and give up but there's always another goal – even if it's just keeping going.

Running brought me more than happiness – it brought me an identity which is something I don't think I had before, except as a teacher. When you feel good about yourself you feel more of a person in your own right. When I started running races people noticed me – perhaps it was because I was an 'older' women and even 20 years ago there weren't that many women of my age running.

It was the one thing that suited me. It fitted in well with my life. But I only knew about running as a 'paper chase' or what elite athletes did but most of all it was boys and men that ran. Women only lurked in the background. We did games at school but never running. Ordinary women didn't run.

In my first race I didn't realise that I was last even when a helpful man offered to run with me but I got such a clap – I thought 'Oooh, I like this. Talk about the roar of the crowd'. And I still didn't realise it was because I was last. I said to my teaching colleagues next day 'Where else do you get clapped like that? They don't clap you at school and your family doesn't clap because you've given them a good meal'.

It was wonderful, heady stuff and I determined to keep going to races.

Because I was old people took a bit of notice of me – old enough to get a bit of respect.

I remember the first time I got 'the high' they talk about. I've only had about three. It's a bit like having a good orgasm, I guess. I remember being on Wimbledon Common on my own and running happily and this lovely feeling that I was mentally, emotionally and physically at one and thinking 'this is what life should really be like – this is what it's all about'. It was only later that I learned about endorphins. Endorphins could be said to be nature's pain killers. Prolonged, continuous exercise contributes to an increased production and release of endorphins, resulting in a sense of euphoria that has been popularly labelled 'runner's high'. Some athletes claim they're addictive – which is what keeps them running. It's a cheap drug, you don't have to pay for it, but if it is a drug you deserve it because you have to work for it.

At the time Britain's top woman marathon runner was, oddly enough, named Joyce Smith. I remember registering for a race and the blokes doing the registration said 'Oh, it's Joyce Smith' and then 'but not THE Joyce Smith.' I said 'Yes but I am Joyce Smith' and they said 'Yes, but you're not THE Joyce Smith, are you?', so it became a joke when friends introduced me and people asked 'are you THE Joyce Smith?' and I became 'the other Joyce Smith'.

When some problem got in the way of my running (particularly my impaired vision which lead to a lot of falls) I just felt frustrated but at the same time I felt that I could overcome the problem. I always felt that if I had to have my legs chopped off

I'd become a wheelchair athlete. Nothing would stop me. It has made me rather hard and unsympathetic to people who give in. I just feel 'why the hell don't they try'. I was brought up that way – my mother was like that. You were either ill in bed or you were up and at school. There was no nonsense.

I had TB in my early 20s and had to lie down for months. My mother couldn't get her head round that. She was very hard on me but I thought 'if I have to live like a bloody cabbage, I'll be a bloody cabbage'. So my body was healing but gosh – up there – in my head there was frustration and determination.

I was sent to a sanatorium in Switzerland for a year. I developed a real love of the mountains as I lay there on the balcony healing in the fresh air. Maybe that was why, when I was 'released', I took up mountain climbing. When the doctor finally said 'You're better now and if you look after yourself, have early nights, start teaching as long as it is just part-time, there's no reason why you shouldn't live as long as the next person'. So I said, 'But I cycle'. 'No, no', he said. 'What about walking?' 'No, no, no, no. Just take it easy!' So I said 'If I don't, what will happen?' 'Well you might see 30', and he showed me to the door. So as I went out I thought 'Now, new pair of boots, new bike', and I was off because I thought 30 was old so I might as well make the most of my last years – I tried to squash the rest of my life in to those few years. Years later I met a girl who'd also been at the sanatorium and taken the doctors advice and she treated herself like an invalid for the rest of her life. I never thought in terms of marriage or children because I was going to die at 30. I'd seen people die in the sanatorium and I believed it would happen to me. I had to go for annual check-ups and it wasn't till I was about 28 when the doctor said I probably didn't need the annual visit that I began to realise I had more years ahead of me. By the time I was 30 I felt secure enough to marry.

In my 40s I developed cataracts and, of course, treatment wasn't as sophisticated as it is now. Later, after I'd started running I got glaucoma. I was prescribed tablets, which I took, but I was fighting the curative effects as I continued running and consequently got tunnel vision. The tablets were slowing me down – they were trying to cure my eyes but because I kept pushing at the running, they didn't do what they should have done but no one explained that to me. I think it just never entered their minds that I was a runner so they wouldn't think to tell me to stop. Maybe, if I'd known the damage I was doing I wouldn't have fought it but I wouldn't have given up running altogether.

So many doctors, including my GP, have said to me 'you must give up running' but they tend to be the older ones. However when I had the TIAs (Transient Ischemic Attacks – mini-strokes) the young doctor said 'Oh no, you carry on running'. It seemed logical – after all, I never had an attack when I was running. They only happened when I was immobile – at a meal or in the theatre.

Before the TIAs I had an aneurism. But there was never any point when I thought I ought to stop. I didn't, and don't, feel frightened. I've already faced death at 30. When you're in your 20s you're very nonchalant about death. I was climbing with a group in North Wales when a member of the party fell to her death. Every bone in her body was broken but even sitting next to her grieving boyfriend after we'd left her in the morgue, it never occurred to me that I should stop climbing mountains. But now that I'm older I would still risk my life to run. I always thought a lovely way to die would be on a podium well into my 80s being given a medal for coming first in my age group in a marathon – everyone is clapping and I just gracefully slip to the ground and they all say 'Ah, how wonderful'. My hair is suddenly a natural colour and all my wrinkles disappear. I'm a vision of serenity.

TAKING CARE OF THE CARER

But now, in my late 70s, I face new kinds of restrictions. My husband has dementia and although he can still be left on his own for short periods of time I have to be an opportunist to seize those moments when he's dozing or watching television to slip out for a short run. I also have to spend more time dealing with the business of our lives, the paperwork that he used to do, and arranging and taking him to medical appointments. My priorities have changed. Previously, running came first and then my domestic duties – now it's the other way around. He knows I have a couple of sacrosanct sessions on Saturday and Sunday mornings when I run with the club. I do feel like I'm being selfish but I also know that it's important that I keep my physical and emotional strength up in order to fulfil my role as a carer. Going out for a run clears your head and puts things in perspective – when you're running you can't worry. Even Ralph says I'm in a better humour when I've been for a run. Carers need some period of their own time to do what they want to do – even if it's just to read a book. It grounds me and makes me feel normal. One of 'them' – not in a grey area – it puts me back in the light. If I didn't run I'd be a very frustrated, bad-tempered old woman. If I couldn't run I'd probably kill myself and him too. There was a very poignant article in *The Guardian* recently, written by a woman whose husband had

Parkinson's and was very disabled by it. She started out describing how she was pushing her husband to church along a coastal path and over a bridge and what a struggle it had been to get him dressed and ready to go out. While she loved him dearly she also lamented the loss of her life as he became more and more confused and dependent on her. I could really empathise with her closing remark 'I look at bridges differently now'.

It's about getting out and doing something that makes you feel good about yourself. It's a continuation of life. I don't run just to pass the time – although it's lovely – it's how I give myself a sense of achievement. My challenge is to make my body – no matter what it's like – work to it's best ability. My life is more worthwhile if I am doing something that results in my achieving something. My latest discovery is aqua-aerobics and although I never learned to swim, I feel so good in the water. I've become an 'aquaholic'. If you can keep your body really fit, it pays off. I love that old saying 'If I'd known I was going to live as long as this I'd have taken better care of myself'.

Ironically I injured my knee doing aqua-aerobics and it's very frustrating because it could take six weeks to get better. I get irritated because I begin to fear that my running days will end and I'd visualised keeping on going at least into my 80s. But at least this injury should get better – it could so easily have been a permanent disability. I am learning to make the best of what life throws at me – that there are limits, boundaries, to what I can do. There was a prisoner who was determined to run a marathon so he trained by running round and round the prison yard and then was allowed out to run the race. He made the best of his circumstances.

DEFINING WOMEN

I've always been able to set myself challenges and take one challenge at a time. For instance, on a walking holiday when I can see a difficult section of road or rock ahead, I say 'Dear God, if I get from here to there I promise I'll only do the easy walk tomorrow' and then I do it and make another pledge for the next challenge and still go out and do the most difficult walk the next day.

We go to a carers group – they're very nice people, all of a certain age. We play reminiscence games and Ralph enjoys it but I don't really want to belong to a group that's mainly based on our ages or where we only have one, depressing thing in common.

That's not my true venue – my true place is with walkers and runners – that's where I feel I belong – where I become the real me. The social aspect of belonging to some multi-generational club or group, like a running or walking club, where you have something in common other than your age (and all the baggage that that carries with it) is so very important. The young (in the club) don't treat me like an old woman. I guess it comes back to my identity. I see myself as a runner so they do too. And now that 'the other Joyce Smith' has faded from most people's memories, I can be the one and only Joyce Smith.

etcetera

Is there a point where seeking independence tips over into selfishness? How do you keep the balance?

Is ageing more difficult for women who's youth has been dominated by some circumstance or ability that is particularly equated with youth (extreme beauty, for instance)?

To what degree is the media responsible for the widespread use of negative stereotypes of older people?

When Joyce recounted the scenario of how she wanted to die (on a podium having just won a medal for running) to a friend, the friend announced that her perfect death would be to eat so many mashed potatoes that she would explode! Match that!

THE ALPHABET CHALLENGE –
THE 'ALPHABIOGRAPHY'

I was asked to write a 100 word (or less) description of myself – what do you choose and what do you leave out? I came up with what I thought was a rather imaginative (and fun) solution – here's my Alphabiography (or should that be a 'biogralphabet'?

Dianne Norton

Amateur/activist/atheist

Bibliophile/Bossy

Cyclist/Canadian/chairman(Wimbledon Light Opera Society)/computer addict/ communicator/CND member

Dianne/dancer/Dragon (born in the year of)

Editor/enthusiast

Friend/foodie/family-fanatic

Grandmother/gym-junkie/graduate/Growing Old Disgracefully member

Hostess/hypochondriac/health-nut

Individual/impatient

Jogger

Kicker-of-butts

Learner/laid-back

Mother/me/managing editor (Third Age Press)/mate

Non-conformist/NIACE member

OAP/outspoken/organiser

Publisher/Political animal/philologist

Rollerblader/rabble-rouser/restless

Singer/socialist/swimmer/skier/shoe maker/ stained glass artist/sister/Scorpio/schadenfreudiste/sixty-six/Sustrans-supporter

Thirdager/tapestry-maker/technophile/tolerant

U3A-founder & member

Vocal/voluptuous

Wife/writer/woman/worrier/Wimbledon Windmiler/www.thirdagepress.co.uk

X (we all need secrets!)

Yoga practitioner

Zesty/zealot

THE ALPHABIOGRAPHY OF
THE RIGHT HONOURABLE ANNE WIDDICOMBE MP

Animal Lover

British

Christian

Devon-bound on retirement

Establishmentarian

Former Shadow Home Secretary

Hardworking

Insistent

Journalist

Kicks compensation culture

Looks after Mother

Novelist

Opposition Front-bencher 1998 - 2001

Pro-lifer

Question Time pundit

Roman Catholic

Safe Haven for Donkeys patron

Tory

University graduate

Vilified by press

Wrinkly

X-rated films not allowed in house

Yearns to end abortion

Zaps political correctness

A donation has been made to Miss Widdicombe's chosen charity ~ **Reason Partnership**® is an international charity dedicated to alleviating the plight of the millions of people in developing countries whose lives are adversely affected by enduring poverty, conflict and natural disasters. According to the WHO, people living in such difficult circumstances are prone not only to epidemics and diseases, but also to severe emotional disturbance which, if left untreated, can lead to severe and enduring mental disorders. Reason Partnership helps communities in such circumstances to rebuild the emotional support systems necessary to maintain and develop healthy communities.   www.reasonpartnership.com

IN THE DARK TIMES WILL THERE STILL BE SINGING?

Frances Marling

On the day that my husband came back with his diagnosis everything became sharp-focused, my mind somehow photographing the scene as though outside it. A daughter had called round and was standing on the stairs and the three of us moved in slow motion. Me to put my arms round him, she to sit down. How archetypal such a moment is, when life has been one thing, with a certain sort of future and then becomes at that moment no longer that but something absolutely other.

He'd felt strange for some time, disorientated and unsteady on his feet. Slowly withdrawing from the world, he took his fear inside. He's never had friends in the way that women have friends.. He readily shares the good times, but the dark times get put elsewhere. At first we had a brief sense of relief that this thing that was happening to him, to us, had a name. Swift to console, the doctor had spoken about the merits of medication, how much better they were now than ever before. How yoga could help to compensate. I'd thought 'it could have been cancer' as I always do. He'd taken early retirement, and had five good years before the illness struck. I had meaningful work, which I loved. I had my practice and was teaching and supervising students, as I still am.

People often have seen my husband as The Man of Fun. It's good to remember that now. Indeed, he still returns to that state whenever he can . It's his nature. He likes to be happy, does not have my compulsion to stagger through life with burdens to carry or problems to be overcome. We slotted in together like hand into glove, he was carefree, I was responsible. Writing this now I see how, at the beginning, we polarised and he acted out the spontaneity and I the caution. Most of my life I had been rather split; the dutiful burdened one would, from time to time, surrender dominance and a Fly Now Pay Later sort of person would leap to the fore – the sort who would have no qualms about leaving this mortal coil with a red wig upon her head, a drawer full of bills, love letters, nearly finished poems, and ten years' dust under the bed. This was the part that envied Edward his freedom to be who he was. But I had my mother's example of a strong sense of duty to restrain me and to keep me more or less on track.

Edward was the fifth and final child of an uncomplicated family in a close-knit community. Everyone seemed to have had their allotted place. His, from what I could see, was to amuse and delight those around him. He was certainly loved and enjoyed by his busy and hard-working parents. His sisters helped their mother in the home at weekends and the boys played with their friends. It seemed like a sort of paradise to me as I heard the family stories and saw how they all related to one another with such acceptance and ease. The child is father to the man and I admired and envied Edward's carefree ways, his sense of fun, maybe even his trust in life. It's what attracted me to him, how different from my depressed and unsociable mother.

Now, observing the dignity with which he laboriously puts on his socks has shamed me into a patience I so rarely feel. He hates his illness, his ever lessening abilities, he fears it too but he also accepts it. Acceptance of what IS seems so simple and yet I've come to value it as a cornerstone for creative living. The capacity to delude oneself is so overriding – to wish rather than to intend. It's said that our destiny is shaped not by our circumstances but our decisions. Freud famously coupled Mourning with Melancholia, or contrasted them rather. To be able to grieve, to mourn, finally to accept over time 'the generous acceptance of inevitable suffering' does, in my experience lead to a sort of freedom, a greater aliveness. So often in my work I see the effect upon an individual of the lack of this capacity. The more or less wasted lives, the inertia of depression, the yearning back to what could have been, of what was lost. All this is a part of the process of mourning of course, I suppose the act of spirit is to struggle out the other side. I've always been drawn to the line 'slouching towards Bethlehem' which humanises and makes more ordinary the heroism of choosing life over death when it seems that all is lost or wrenched away.

The early days of our marriage were the best of times and the worst of times. Our warm, chaotic family life gradually unfroze and enlivened me. Edward knew about babies and longed for a family of his own. Between us we provided colour, fun and tangled confusion for our beloved children. He was a natural, I had to learn every step

of the way. What he instinctively knew about people and life I had no experience of. I had gleaned the little I did know from brief, intensely observed visits to schoolfriends' homes and none of them had younger siblings. English parents were so much more formal then and I could get few clues or inspirations from them about the real life I so desperately sought. I must have carried however, a tiny intense treasure hidden within the knapsack of my particular presenting past.

I see that now, as a sort of inner blueprint – one that I could not yet decipher but which was to lead me, directly and indirectly to seek, and eventually to find, what I needed and longed for. But that was later, much later. I realised early on in our marriage that Edward's path outside the home was one that I would rarely share. That he would continue to walk on his own path. At first this disturbed me deeply, I felt left behind, sometimes abandoned. It was certainly not what I would have chosen, this independence that I felt was forced upon me. But the price, which at first felt so high, was paid at the beginning. I can see from my present perspective that I shall probably reap the rewards for the rest of my life. Then, I knew so little of how marriages worked. That came later by observing my friends, who did not seem to do it the way we were doing it. But then, in my early days my imprint was of living without a father, and of a mother who coped, or did not cope by herself. It was my blindspot. I didn't know about making demands, calling the tunes. It seemed that a path was laid out for me which I reluctantly took. As much as I was disappointed to find that I felt so alone again, I was, I'm quite sure, not surprised.

I see now that Edward was simply following his own pattern, as I was following mine. Boys became men. Men still had

DEFINING WOMEN

friends whom they did things with. Women had different lives, and had their children, sisters, mothers. Carrying my awkwardness with me I gradually found friends of my own, wherever I looked. Ones who generously shared their lives with me, as did I with them. Ones who could have peopled my earliest fantasies of all that life could hold. With nearly all of them we are friends still. I steeped myself in crafts, and took up the strands of my early interests and studies. Edward worked to support us and I was grateful for that. It gave me the space and the time to learn, at last, to play. I tried on ways of being in exactly the way that I would put paper outfits on cardboard cut-out people as a child. A particular memory comes of when I hennaed my hair, wore Hindu Kush dresses and thought myself, timid thirty-year-old mother of three, to be a hippy.

Edward's capacity to amuse and delight has never left him. His fine eye for the absurd enabled us to transcend many of our difficulties. He remains the one person who has ever reduced me to tears of laughter. 'There's more to life than having fun' my mother would say. I can't argue with the truth of that but it was a unitive experience that gave us all far more than temporary happiness. As a family, humour seems now to be among our favourite values. So, there were our lives together, and our lives apart. Only later did I see how much that had come to serve me .The interests which Edward and I were to develop were, in fact, so different. The bond which grew between us was not formed, therefore, from shared interests but shared values.

At the core of both our value systems was a need for freedom, to be who we really are, to go where we really wanted. Had Edward been like the men I saw around me, the men of the 'doing things together couples' I could so easily have rested in the happiness I longed for, not in the search for meaning and fulfilment that I then pursued. It only gradually dawned upon me that the freedom to branch out, to allow myself to follow my inner blueprint, when I eventually found it, was, in fact, what I had always needed. In a sense we each provided a more or less secure base for one another, from which we both thereafter walked on different paths and at different paces.

When, through affection or good manners, we walked together I would lengthen my stride to his. Being tall he had a long stride. I'm glad now to look back and see how much he enjoyed walking off into his own world, being his own man, doing what he wanted to do. I also see that so many of the events of my life which were on the cutting edge of my known experience, certainly well beyond the realms of comfortable ease, were the ones that I later found so rewarding. They challenged me so utterly that I would probably not have undertaken them had he agreed to come with me into my world. It is easy for me to envy couples who do share huge parts of their outer lives. I project into their relationships an interest in one another, in the heart of who they really are. I longed always for Edward to be interested in the me I take myself to be. I have had to accept that he isn't. But to see also that he has made no attempt to change me, to wish me to be other than I am. I was never in doubt that he loves me. I have had to reassess many times over the years my definitions of love. Over lunch in the garden he said one day 'How lucky I am to have such a lovely, imaginative and clever wife'. We rarely send cards or give flowers. It was the first time in all those years that he has ever said such a thing. 'I often think it', he said, 'I just don't think to say it'.

Now we shuffle together. He takes my arm or I take his. Sometimes I like the comfort of it. At those times it reminds me of those little plastic people our children used to play with attached to a weight by a string. His hands on her hips they would walk in single file, leaning to the left, leaning to the right, shuffle, shuffle to the edge of the table. And I still have the choice of strides, of paths. I can dash off here, slowly explore there, alone or with friends but when together he and I now take the wide, well-trodden footways where obstacles will not trip us up. The foreign vistas have gone, and that's alright. We have a hut in the garden where the view is a gentle and a small one. We can watch the crows building and

clambering around their untidy nest high in a neighbouring tree. At the beginning this hut in the garden was my retreat. Now we share it. We eat lunch in there often. Sometimes I sleep in there between morning and afternoon work. The best times are candlelit suppers on a thundery summer evening, the huge splodges of rain so comforting on the roof, the lightning exciting, like all wild dissonances and breakings up of complacent harmonies.

I've often noticed that to tell one's story, to find a narrative for one's life, is a healing affair. Maybe over time Edward will find and write his story, his version of his life, with and without me. This is mine.

DEFINING WOMEN

Writing, finding the right words to say it, leaves me feeling like the harvest hymn 'all is safely gathered in, free from sorrow, free from sin'. Or, perhaps more accurately sins and sorrows become a part of the rich weft and web of a life. The tangled masses of unstoried experiences are like the great aunts' knitting bags. In separating and regrouping the colours my life becomes more meaningful, revealing connections and insights as I unpick, sort and roll up the new balls. I find to my surprise that, however discordant the colours or ill-matched the threads had seemed to be at first, nothing is wasted. For this to work I have had to learn to think in a different sort of way. It has taken slowness, silence and solitude to truly engage with and make sense of inner and outer experience. To undergo experience neither evading it nor being defeated by it. Simone Weil said once that the false god turns suffering to violence and the true god turns violence to suffering. There is something about that word, to suffer, to bear, one's experience that has been important to me. Over time it's enabled me to realise that, if I can find a way to simply be with whatever life presents, and listen to the truth of my feelings and thoughts about it, however painful it is, the experience changes. It then holds a quality of aliveness in it. Simply sitting with the feelings that arise does not add to the suffering, they actually come into focus, move through and leave. But I have to be truthful. I can no longer deceive myself about my motives, my feelings or how I would like others to see me. It is clear to me now how exhausting my old self-deceptions and shoring up of hopes and images have always been. So many paradoxes lie in this newer, freer way. My old ways were to paint a brighter picture than the reality I was feeling. I discovered almost accidentally that if I, literally and metaphorically,

paint out a dream or a dark inner state as accurately as possible, however painful, it has the extraordinary effect of relief and a sort of self-respecting spaciousness. In this place the new can arise. And it often does, although the relief and spaciousness feel enough in themselves. Like a sense of the calm after the storm.

One of the mysteries of life seems to me that there are trustworthy rules, mentors and teachers wherever I have longed to find them. I have searched them out and been truly grateful for their generosity and wisdom. And still I have gone my own way, following the deeply etched patterns laid out for me in my early childhood. So it wasn't my way at all, it was running like a train on automatic lines, reacting to signals of 'Stop 'and 'Danger Ahead', as though the danger was now and the person I am now is the person I was then. I found myself to be a converter, a restorer rather than a tearer down of the obsolete and an innovative rebuilder. I lacked the courage to protest and didn't know how to demand. I became the sort of person who stole from the backdoor rather than overtly asking at the front. So this is a little of my story of our life together, and my life apart. Of how I have felt and how I see it now. It's a story of the repeating of patterns, of findings and dispossesions, and of making new paths.

Edward's news had come at the end of a year of losses. Some seemed to me to be self-destructive acts that people I love were embarking upon, others were unpreventable. Having to bear, without the capacity to influence, is never easy. In my work people come to me wishing to find a better way through their lives. That year I felt like Cassandra, blessed with all that I thought I knew but finding myself faced with the unresponding eye, with the head that turns away. Like April to the poet, hope had become my cruelest month.

Like many children who lose a parent very young my great vulnerability has always been to loss and, in the curious way that such things can happen, having the flood-gates forced open again I was carried on a tide that year that bore me backwards through my life to experience the depths and roots of all old sorrows, terrors and emptinesses. I landed, as a two-year-old at the shores of my father's death. I found the seed thought, during that experience, that unconsciously had become a haunting sort of leitmotif during my life at all periods of dark change, 'my life is now over . . .'. Writing about it now it seems suddenly to be an over-indulgence, a Marie-Antoinette amongst her sheep sort of self-absorption. When I'm in that state it is shiveringly hollow, isolating, gobbling up of hope. Real contact with others is severed, as it is with the outside world, and with myself. Since that year of losses I now see very clearly that the two-year old inside me, at those times, reigns supreme.

My hardest times now are when I feel ill or when, as was the case this spring, I injured my back. To realise so starkly that our well-being rests upon my back had been a shock. Vulnerable and miserable I wanted to give up the struggle, to lie under the duvet and weep. I wanted to be looked after, cheered up and indulged with songs. Lamentations and dirges would have been the most consoling of songs. Edward used to be our singer of songs. The pain cocoon I was in did bring insights and connections which I could never have gained in other ways. I saw how fragile my hold on reality is, how I see everything through the eyes of my present state as though it would last for ever. Life had become, suddenly, utterly restricted. I was flung back to the earliest of times yet again, stifled with hopelessness, reliving old feelings of powerlessness and how it had been to be 'stuck at home with a depressed mother'. Optimism and imagination fled. I looked at our ancient dog and felt how cruel it was to keep him in what I could only see as his suffering, his aching joints, his trembling gait. 'After all, it's the one thing we can give him, to let him not suffer', I'd thought. I fell into this state more than surrendered to it. But I did bear it and then the changing moment came when I woke one morning with the knowledge that something very old had turned into its opposite. I realised absolutely, and possibly for the first time, that I was not an impotent child – that I was an autonomous and sociable adult and that there was a life that awaited me. I saw the dog clearly and without the projections of my death-dealing eye, marvelling at his delight in the early spring sweetness of the outside world as he staggered forth to cover every other dog smell with that of his own.

It was also valuable to find a kinder voice in me which told me that independence could now be lessened, that I could change the patterns a little. During those weeks I learned to seek and find help, to ask to be cheered up and to find ears that the most secret, ancient and isolated part of me could whisper into. That there was no point in demanding salt from someone who sold butter, but to find a purveyor of salt. And to find there were still singers of songs. Again, though, I wonder whether darkness doesn't always sit as a foundation for the light? And happiness, what of happiness? There is now a long-overdue and serious study of the science of happiness. Neuroscience has sobering proof that optimal left brain development happens within the first three years of life. This is our social brain, and the seat of our cheerfulness. But the brain retains a certain plasticy and new connections between the right and left hemispheres can, to a certain degree, make up their losses, enabling what has been lost to mind to return to mind. It has been discovered, as we all surely instinctively know, that the love, empathy and acceptance of others enables emotional and intellectual growth. This is a slow process, but it gives true hope, and it involves telling one's story, finding the meaning that is so hard for the right brain function to conceptualise and put into words. So, can we learn to be happy? I suspect that there is a wider gap than we may realise between what we want and what makes us happy.

I have come to recognise that in my old dread-filled days, spawned in ancestral and childhood hauntings, there simply wasn't room for much beyond those fears and dreads. Consciously I'm sure I presented myself as a somewhat brittle optimist. Inside there was little real hope. The journey I took so reluctantly has reaped rich rewards in that, along the way, it has cleared away the ghosts, both my own and those inherited from parents, grandparents, even great-grandparents, as family myths have shown me. I can stand in the present moment uncluttered by old detritus, unfettered by no-longer-believed-in stories. I have not rebuilt the railway, but I have, piece by piece, laid a new track. And I have a profound respect for life and those who live it. I see as much beauty as I do darkness and have a sense of awe and grace in the human condition. I can accept now in a way quite impossible before, that I am regularly seized by moods of resentment, spite and fury when my heroic attempts to hold everything together fail to get the acknowledgement I feel they so richly deserve. And I can also laugh at myself as well as feel real pity for both of us when I'm particularly cruel. There are no rules for what we both face now. As in the early days of our marriage we have to make it up as we go along. But we both love the good times when I can relax, let chaos reign, allow the dust to settle, and return to cheerfulness. At one again with the god of things as they are.

I used to have a fantasy that the hating side of love was so bad that I would be cast out if all those dark feelings were to be known. I caught them only out of the corner of my own eye, I certainly hid them from the eyes of others. It has been a relief to reveal the whole gamut of who I am, to others, and to myself. The friends who loved me do so still for who, not what, I am and we can be increasingly truthful with one another. Edward has shown me the way in this. He is an honest self-accepting and loving man. Kipling had introduced me to this new god, the one of things as they are, which is the first god I have ever come to worship. 'Each in his separate star shall draw the thing as he sees it, for the God of Things as they are'. It is there that I have found happiness. Not the pleasure of circumstances, but moments of transcendent joy. The fact that this is a state which does not depend upon anything turning out a particular way seems rather miraculous to me as I write. For that is the point of it. If I know that I can be, with whatever feeling arises in me, and bear it, I no longer need to dread particular events that in the past would have flung me into shame, grief or fear.

And to find that it is the very experiencing of such a wide gamut of emotions, if I don't judge them as good or bad, that brings richness and colour to my life. The early past can become the dark backcloth against which the light of a new order can now be seen. And the freedom of this state seems to be what has led me to experience happiness whenever it does arise. And knowing what makes me happy I can simply do it more!

Frances Marling

So many of the patterns I brought into my adult life, and which compelled me to comply rather than protest, were born out of my childhood fears of my mother. The often sweet and natural woman that she later became as she, too, was warmed by the company and affection of all her grandchildren was not the mother of my earliest days. Then, I found her unreachably distant and was especially afraid of the silences between us. I had recurrent nightmares as a child of looking for my reflection in her dressing-table mirror and there being no-one there. The 'no-one there' where I should have been was utterly, hauntingly terrifying. Like the discovery of the endless unbeing of death. Now I feel that I understand her, the privations of her life after my father's death, her thrift and endurance, I even sense a silent brooding sort of devotion, to both my brother and me which she was unable to express. She, too, hadn't yet learned about love and how to do it. She had turned her back on life, and was very alone. Now I can look into that dressing-table mirror, in my imagination and see us both, her dignity and strength, me so like her but sturdier and more in touch with joy. And I am proud of her. And I glimpse a sense that she is proud of me, that she approves my growing beyond the constraints she imposed. That she and my ancestry of bereft and grieving women somehow nod and smile at me for undertaking the quest, and passing the test. In redeeming my past it seems to me that these solitary women become a little less alone. That a tide floods back over the generations shifting and changing ancestral patterns, softening memories and freeing those ancient voices to find their own words, and to sing their dark songs. We belong to one another and, if a surprising joy falls on me, then maybe it blesses us all.

etcetera

Is being able to turn 'suffering' into a positive experience the true test of surviving? *'Older people share with those of all ages the desire for fulfilment – a need to transform surviving into thriving'*. What strategies have you found for exploring painful situations and turning them into positive challenges?

Dignity and freedom is knowing when and how to ask for help. Can a fierce (and stubborn) independence be confining rather than liberating if we don't acknowledge its limits.?

Is a bond based on shared values more enduring than one based on shared interests?

* Yvonne Craig, editor , **'Changes and Challenges in Later Life: learning from experience'** published by Third Age Press. Details on page 152.

MRS SLATER

Maggie Guillon

Mrs Slater takes in other people's ironing. She only lives two doors away but I wouldn't let her loose on my sheets, pushing and prodding at them with those clammy fingers and poking her sharp little nose into my underwear. Somehow I'm convinced that they would come back grey and have to be washed all over again.

Because everything about Mrs Slater is grey. Her windows and curtains are grey from a coating of daily steam. Her skin has a dull, pallid quality that you wouldn't really expect on someone who spends most of the time in her own small sauna. Her hair is grey, not so much from age as from years of neglect, and her wardrobe, such as it is, seems to have been carefully selected to match. Nothing about her has the slightest suggestion of charm.

Thump, hiss, thump – her face is blunt with indifference as she pounds away at a pile of cheerful shirts in dreary silence. I glance at her through the fusty glass as I pass by, always grateful that she is still indoors and not waiting at the gate for a new delivery. There is nothing more disheartening than a damp 'Mornin' from drab Mrs Slater on an overcast day.

Sometimes I stand behind her in the corner shop on a Friday afternoon. She buys a packet of Rich Tea Fingers and some PG Tips teabags. Oh, and something to prevent lime scale in the iron. Every Friday. In her long grey coat. Grey Mrs Slater and her grey, grey life.

But this morning she is standing in her room, motionless. I can see her slightly bent over the ironing board but her arms are hanging down and the iron sits upright and alone on the stand. Through the droplets running down the pane her shape alters and swells, shakes a little then shrinks again, and there is a sound, a strange muffled sound coming from the house.

On an impulse – call it good neighbourliness if you will – I open the flaking gate and walk up the short driveway to the front window. Her back is to me so I peer in, and just as I do so she turns her face towards me. It is wet with steam and tears and contorted into a kind of ecstasy, and somewhere in that dark little room I can hear the aching strains of Puccini's *O Mio Babbino Caro'*

Mrs. Slater dreams in colour.

etcetera

Never judge a book by its cover . . . things – and certainly people – aren't always what they seem.

How would you describe the chasm between the person others see and your own inner self? Are there any advantages in trying to close the gap between the two?

As we age, do we become more finely tuned to the vulnerabilities of people behind their outer persona? How do we learn to read between the lines?

A NEW DEPARTURE

Dorothy Underwood

Call it the wind of change, but during the last decade there has been a growing interest in obituaries possibly caused by the public reaction at the funeral of Princess Diana when Earl Spencer spoke with such conviction at Westminster Abbey.

It was therefore no surprise to me when invited to a literary evening called 'Desert Island Books', to hear a well known author say that one of the books that she would choose to take with her were she marooned would be 'The Daily Telegraph Book of Obituaries' – celebration of eccentric lives. Hence the fictional Frogmorton.

Eulogies can sometimes be dull and monotonous if one takes the usual route – childhood, work, retirement. The alternative can be to lighten the situation as did the employee asked to pay tribute to a domineering, blasphemous, hard-drinking Scrooge-like skinflint, by saying, 'Mr Morpeth was respectful, discriminating and vociferous . . . respectful of time, as those of us who worked for him knew; discriminating in the fact that he had few friends; vociferous – not unfamiliar with the use of strong language – we shall miss him'.

Perhaps you have been invited to write or say something about the life of a close relative. A eulogy can be an interesting short story – an abbreviated account of a life – both informative and heartening.

OBITUARY
Fenella Fotheringay Fortesque Frogmorton

Clairvoyant and Speech Writer

One of the twentieth century's most colourful literary eccentrics has died at her home in Wimbledon. Her age – a closely guarded secret. Frogie, as she liked to be called, was also a woman of acute business acumen.

She practiced from her well-appointed apartment on The Ridgeway. Her clients were among the rich and famous from all over the world: Actors, Politicians, Artists, Royalty, Pop Stars – those on their way up and those on their way down. All eager to know what Fate had in store.

She displayed a surprising knowledge of a wide variety of subjects, and had the latest books in her large library.

Miss FFFFw was a caustic critic at public meetings and very active in local affairs – when finally Wimbledon Tennis welcomes its much-needed sliding roof it will be to Frogie's ardent campaigning to which the fans should be grateful.

She was the source of numerous anecdotes and enjoyed being part of a closely-knit coterie of clairvoyants and writers, but it was not until well into middle age that she began her much lesser known and far more lucrative activity, that of speech writing, which she ran concurrently with clairvoyance.

It all began with a simple advertisement in *The Times*. 'Allow me to write your speech for you, tailored to suit your personality and that of your audience. Informal groups to large gatherings' ex. refs. She was inundated – and so began a place in history to which few could aspire.

Literally the voice behind the throne, but a voice that always remained silent, for above all she was a woman of the highest integrity, discreet and respectful, assuring her clients that the utmost secrecy would prevail at all times. She would be the source of towering unforgettable orations, or, when appropriate, a simple sincere eulogy for a Funeral – a tribute to a loved one. She also had a delightful sense of humour which could lighten an otherwise dull atmosphere, sometimes bordering on satire, but never facetious – invaluable to the chairman of large companies at senior staff level, for retirement parties or after-dinner speeches.

She likened herself to a good cook – all she needed were a few raw ingredients, basic facts from which she would build a memorable speech.

When reading her obituary many public figures will feel a certain unease at her passing. Will their well-known words now be revealed to have flowed from the pen of Frogie? Might there now be a book of FFFF memoirs – revealing all – The Biography of Fennela Fotheringay Fortesque Frogmorton?

Such fears will be ungrounded for her last wish was that her work should remain anonymous, she was in the truest sense a ghostwriter.

Her only indulgence was listening to recordings of famous speeches which one could hear while waiting to have one's fortune told.

She has no survivors.

etcetera

The life of every man is a diary in which he means to write one story, and writes another, and his humblest hour is when he compares the volume as it is with what he vowed to make it. J M Barrie, novelist and playwright (1860-1937)

Write an obituary of the person you wish you'd been – or write several from different points of view (your child, sibling, spouse, friends, fellow students, work and/or playmates).

The Daily Telegraph Book of Obituaries: a celebration of eccentric lives edited by Hugh Massingberd

Chin Up, Girls!: A Book of Women's Obituaries from the Daily Telegraph by Georgia Powell, Katharine Ramsay

SOME DAY I'LL GO TO MOGADOR

Dianne Norton

Part way along the A217, between the M25 and Sutton in Surrey, there's a sign pointing down a narrow road reading 'Mogador'. For years, every time I've driven past it, I've wondered about Mogador – it sounds like something out of a Daphne du Maurier novel – remote and mysterious – and promised myself that someday I'd turn left instead of travelling straight on and home.

Imagine my amazement when, a couple of years ago, on Wimbledon Station, returning from a night out in London, I happened to overhear a woman say to her two companions, 'I've always been curious about Mogador – some day I'm going to go there'. I should have tapped her on the shoulder and compared fantasies, but I didn't – I went straight on and home.

The last time I drove past the signpost it reminded me of the Robert Frost poem, 'The Road Not Taken', that is carved, as he had chosen, on the memorial to my father. 'Two roads diverged in a wood and I, I took the one least travelled by, and that has made all the difference.' But I digress . . . but surely that's the point . . . I don't digress.

What difference might it make to my life if I went to Mogador? How many other signposts have I driven by in the past 65 years that might have made a difference had I but turned off the well-travelled road?

Travelling through life could be likened to playing a board game. You move along the given squares until some act of fate (a roll of the dice) diverts you on to another path – Snakes and Ladders for real. Or is it more like a pinball machine where we're propelled out of a starting gate and proceed to career around the 'playing field' changing direction every time an obstacle gets in our way? If life were like that particular game we would never have the option of climbing over an obstacle when it got in our way.

Recalling my (and millions of others') fascination with I Ching in the 60s, (but being unable to recall exactly how it worked), I went onto the internet and to Google and started searching. So many references, so many tracks, so many roads down which one could wander and then find oneself at yet another group of forks where a decision was necessary. How do I choose which will yield the most/best knowledge? But wasn't that what I Ching was all about – making those random choices about life? Is Google a virtual road to Mogador?

Wandering through the vast London International Book Fair at Olympia on a hot and dusty day a few years ago I began to feel that my weary eyes were playing tricks on me. I was looking for a specific stand and as I searched for it in a labyrinth of books I noticed that a sign saying 'new' books actually said 'few' books the next time I passed it. Three times I consulted the map board to see where my chosen destination was and three times I set off only to find it was the wrong place – every time the map seemed to say something different. I later discovered that it was the map that was incorrect – not me – but by this time I was seriously beginning to think something was happening to my brain. I fled. Outside, away from the harsh flourescent lights and the heat and babble of thousands of people I felt instantly better but realised how tired I was so hopped on the train for home only to find it was the wrong train.

The train went to Willesden Junction and as I stepped out on the platform (in order to wait for a train back in the opposite direction and home) I was greeted with an extraordinary sight but one that presumably thousands of people walk by every day. The platform is perched high over the urban landscape. On one side unremarkable terraced houses form a compact suburb. On the other is the junction – a complex network of train tracks crossing and crisscrossing each other and beyond that, the biggest scrap yard I had ever seen. Mountains of old and rusty cars were piled up waiting their fate. How many wrong turns had those cars taken in their time? How many life changing moments had they played a part in? How many deaths or maybe even births?

But the thing that really drew my eyes in that scene was a monumental, fire-belching car-crushing plant into which these sad old motors were waiting to be fed, to be turned into something else. It brought to mind a scene from an otherwise forgotten film in which a man who had more money than he knew what to do with, bought a new Rolls Royce and had it crushed into a rectangle which he then kept on view in his apart-

ment. So if fate leads us into a situation where we are transformed into something else – is that necessarily a bad thing? Could we come out as a work of art?

Meanwhile back in Willesden my other reaction was that this would make a perfect site for a baddies vs goodies chase in a James Bond movie. I could just imagine Sean Connery (who else for a woman of my age?) scaling metal ladders inside the plant, hotly pursued by the evil villain only to be caught and engaged in a life or death struggle while dangling over the fiery furnace.

Apart from giving my imagination a rather exciting day out, did taking the wrong train that day really change my life? Probably not in any substantial way but the very fact that I am writing this piece obviously demonstrates what an impact it had on me. And it has changed the way I looked at London. It made me realise that the city is full of unusual, dramatic and colourful places that are definitely not on the tourist map and as long as we continue to take the more travelled roads we'll miss them. I've contemplated taking visitors from abroad to Willesden station just to show them what a vibrant place it is. But like Mogador, I've never done it.

Now you may be beginning to think that I'm not really a very adventurous person – that I just let life roll along and bring me whatever it will although I obviously appreciate the stimulation of a new experience when it falls into my lap.

Maybe that's the important thing – not whether or not we go looking for new and life-changing experiences but rather what we do with those experiences when they come our way. Is that what makes the seemingly wrong road into the right one – an attitude of mind?

Like a lot of married couples, my husband and I have arguments when travelling in the car. I particularly remember one where he finally shouted at me, 'Doesn't the U3A do map reading courses?' He claims, quite rightly, that I can't read a map. If he's driving he gets agitated when we get lost. I've discovered that, when visiting a place we've never been before, it is much better if I drive and he reads the map – because I don't get my knickers in a twist when we go astray (although I do when I'm on my own and in a hurry and have no one to blame but myself. At least with my husband I can blame him for driving so fast that I can't see the road signs!). It may be that I have more of a sense of adventure than he does and have taken enough wrong turnings to appreciate that something interesting can result from getting lost. Or it may be that I am more prepared to admit that I can't read a map – a failing he would never admit to. Or it might even be something to do with the alleged different 'wiring' in men's and women's brains that results in different spatial awareness abilities.

I appreciate that I have written here about what may be two quite different phenomena: I see an avenue that intrigues me but don't take it; or, I accidentally take an incorrect turning and enjoy the experience it leads me to. This probably tells you a lot more about me as a person than it does about the phenomenon of 'fate'.

Dianne Norton

Miles of books have been written about 'fate' and 'destiny' and about whether they are the same thing or not. Obviously the word 'destiny' seems more closely related to 'destination' than does the word 'fate'. (A quick and simplistic divider might be that fate is a power whereas destiny is an end product – a destination). My purpose is not to add to this discussion but rather to set the reader on a journey of thought just as I have been myself.

I certainly don't want to get into a discussion about the involvement of a 'higher power' although I will lay my cards on the table and say that, personally, I think it possible that we use words like 'fate' and 'destiny' because we frail humans need explanations where none exist.

Which brings us back to my personal dilemma. Why, if I am aware of enjoying the consequences of my 'wrong turnings', do I not deliberately seek them out and go in search of my Mogador? Could it be that if the result of going off the beaten track was disappointing, then I would have only myself to blame? Whereas, if by chance, I have a bad experience, it wouldn't be my fault (Oh, I know – I could have taken more care to get on the 'right' train). Or is my life full and satisfying enough that I only need to be able to let my imagination run wild without having, physically, to pursue those challenges? I can control my mind but might not be able to control what happened to me if I turned left down that road to Mogador. Some of the answer may have to do with time. Admittedly, whenever I pass that crossroad to Mogador I am on my way to or from somewhere else. If I had more time would I be more adventurous? I used to work with a woman who, although I didn't know her well, seemed rather timid

and certainly not outgoing. But I was told by a colleague that when she retired she set about travelling around London on every bus in numerical sequence – that is, starting with bus route No. 1 (which, by the way, aptly starts at Centre Point) through to No. 895 (which ends up in the Great Western Industrial Park in Southall - who know, perhaps it's as inspiring as Willesden Junction). What a great idea – just think of all the places you'd see and people you'd meet - not to mention keeping warm in winter and not having to expend too much energy and it would be completely free! But, come to think of it, the only chance there would be for 'fate' to intervene would be in who were cast as your fellow passengers and if any accident (or road works) intervened to cause the bus to divert from its' normal route. I think I do crave more excitement than that.

So is it about control and balance? People probably don't choose to be 'control freaks', do they? Nor do most of us want to be constantly buffeted by the winds of fate (or should that be destiny?). A happy medium is what we're after – the freedom to choose whether or not we follow fate or, at other times, enjoy the titillation of wondering what might have been if only . . .

But sometimes, just sometimes, there are things that it's important to believe were meant to be. In the exquisitely beautiful and painful prose poem/novel by Elizabeth Smart, *By Grand Central Station I Sat Down and Wept* she expresses thus the inevitability of her fall into love: '*I stand on the edge of the cliff, but the future is already done. It is written. Nothing can escape . . . For me there was no choice. There were no crossroads at all*'.

Do you have a 'road to Mogador'?

Oxford English Dictionary: **Fate:** *'development of events outside a person's control, regarded as predetermined by a supernatural power'*

Destiny: *'the events that will necessarily happen to a particular person in the future'* . . . then who controls our destiny?

A person often meets his destiny on the road he took to avoid it. ~ Jean de La Fontaine

You have to leave the city of your comfort and go into the wilderness of your intuition. What you'll discover will be wonderful. What you'll discover is yourself. ~ Alan Alda

If you don't get lost, there's a chance you may never be found. ~ Author Unknown

I may not have gone where I intended to go, but I think I have ended up where I intended to be. ~ Douglas Adams

RIDING THE CAROUSEL

Hilary Elfick

I learnt the truth of taking life by the horns somewhere around my mid fifties.

I had spent most of my life by a carousel. Sometimes I sat where I was put, watching the people clambering up, riding, swooping up and down. I followed their progress, then half-closed my eyes so that they blurred. Sometimes I became involved, running from one horse to another, lifting people on and off, or helping them stay on. What I didn't seem to have done for a long time was to get on a horse myself, with no one to help me. People would be scandalised; my husband had once said a woman should never lose her dignity. But it would be another way to simply find out how it was done. My two year old granddaughter says firmly 'I do it.' Right. That's the starting point.

There were two catalysts.

I had buried the fourth of our parents, and our children had gone – one on a gap year, the others already working. My husband was looking forward to retirement, in which he threatened to take over domestic management. (And why should that be a threat? Sounds good to me now!) He had spent long periods working away from home, and our communication, though mostly amiable, was poor. He and I were hugely supportive of our kids' courage, in travel to the Far East, the Antipodes, Africa, the USA, in experiences I'd never

had. It dawned on me that my recently lost parents had once been like that for me. I began to feel like a teenager – longing to leave home and get out there.

And then one day I had been demonstrating the art of Saxon building to a class of 7 year-olds, bare-foot treading the daub (water, hair, manure, clay) and then hurling it (mud-slinging of course) while shouting the name of my most deadly enemy, when one boy said 'Mrs Elfick's too old to behave like this.'

Who was my most deadly enemy? My most deadly enemy was that I was what I was expected to be. And it was my own fault. I had not surprised anyone for a long time. I needed a gap year. I needed to get over the fact that I probably wouldn't get permission.

At 55 I had never hired a car for myself. I had never travelled completely alone. I had never been out of range, never been where absolutely no one knew where I was.

Now what you need to understand is that I am a wimp. If you are the kind of wife who always had a strong sense of identity, who got out there and amazed your family as a matter of routine, this is not for you. For years I had always been on my way somewhere, always hurrying, frequently hanging about waiting – but for other people.

My enemies were without (neglecting her duties) and within (but what if?) Neither of those was actually valid. Finding this out was the adventure, the discovery.

Using a small but sufficient legacy from my parents, I took my gap year. Permission came when it became quite clear that I would go anyway. My family wanted me to leave as many anchor points as possible of where I was, and of course it's only responsible that someone should be able to contact you within a few days if the family needs to. But I realised that part of the point of this is to do it alone, and to let go of the links, to learn how to swim, how to trust the water to hold you up. And I didn't want an itinerary. I wanted to be able to respond to place, to opportunity.

I felt that year that I needed to draw a veil over myself as a woman throws a damp cloth over the rising dough, or even as a pilgrim goes veiled so she can press on. People, like reporters, want stories, especially from travellers, and if you give them stories about the way ahead, or even the way you have come before you understand it yourself, then you either end up like an actor with a script, trying to be consistent (in line with what you've led them to expect) or you arouse their consternation by living out an unfolding story which does not match what you said, and is not the situation to which, in all good faith, they have adjusted. Yet only that which is living can adapt and grow, and that means change.

But I don't just mean pockets of space. Nor do I mean wanting to write uninterrupted, for writing is what I do. I realised I meant more than that, and it was there that I most offended. 'Shouldn't she be taken out of herself?' my friends and family muttered – yes, and that is exactly what they wanted to do! The silence, the apparent prepara-

tory inactivity, the brooding (but let them look at the origin of the metaphor 'brooding'!) seemed such a concern to others, yet its heart and its jewel was the depth and length and quality of solitude for its own sake that I craved, and it was that which others found so hard to grasp or forgive. They read it as rejection, and even to outsiders it was immensely threatening. One day, half way through my great escape, a woman's husband said to me, pointing his finger – 'You, Madam, are a very dangerous woman!'

'And will she ever come back?' I couldn't answer that either. Not honestly. All I could say was that if I did come back it would be because I wanted to.

Picture that carousel. You need to be strapped to the horse. Past memories are the Sirens which call to you. The role you have played in the family is now under severe threat. Some of the calls may not be Sirens at all, but authentic cries, and you will not be able to tell one from the other.

Going into the wilderness is not easy for a 54 year old woman who has the human and practical links I have. When the wilderness (and how deeply I love that word!) is invaded by the friendly or unfriendly, the veil goes on. People find it hard to live with our 'I don't know', harder to live with 'I'm not saying'. All I knew is that I was walking ahead of me and that in the long periods of silence nothing seemed to be happening – but I could breathe.

The core of my gap year was nine months in Australia and New Zealand, but I also went alone to Kenya and Uganda. When I did it, I encountered and recorded the largest Eastern brown snake ever known in New South Wales (one of the Big Ten for fast and nasty death), a shotgun-happy drug grower in the bush, and had the rarest bird in the world accompany me on a

DEFINING WOMEN

walk and peck my boot. I jet-boated up a rocky wilderness river, landed by helicopter on a glacier, and steered an enormous old square rigger under Sydney Harbour Bridge. I was surrounded by drunk, trigger happy black police when I lost my way in the back streets of Nairobi and was embraced in the Eastern highlands of Zimbabwe by a black singer who had never hugged a white person before. I knelt in the dust with a dying woman in a Ugandan prison, and in a roundel with a small boy with only hours to live. I faced out a man who became suddenly violent in a cedar house in a remote lane, and swam with a Groper fish as large as myself.

I learnt to handle anything that was alive, and to kill when there was no alternative.

Did I ever panic? Of course I did. Driving on an unknown track in Tasmania,

cramped by diarrhoea, nowhere to stay, I kept hearing in my head Kipling's lines

Ere Mor the Peacock flutters
Ere the Monkey People cry
Ere Chil the Kite swoops down a
Through the Jungle very softly
flits a shadow and a sigh ---
He is Fear, O little Hunter, he is
Fear.

I was often very scared indeed, and occasionally with good reason. At other times it was just the raw 'How on earth did I get here from there?' – there being the world I had left behind me.

But a great gift was that I met a surprising number of people who were doing what I was, and facing the same fears. The difference was that I was female and nearly forty years older than they were. There is,

Hilary Elfick

I discovered, an advantage in that. Short legs, white hair, a female without make-up or jewellery, I threatened no one out in deserted places, and I was no bait for the odd predatory male. Of course they existed. But the strangest people gave me good tips. One was Audrey who recounted the tale of dealing with a stranded motorist very late one night. There have been at times way-ward travellers who hide out in the Bush, sometimes drug dealers so she was rather nervous, and she described how she whis-pered to this motorist that her drunk and violent husband was asleep in the house and must on no account be woken, and brought him out a blanket so he slept out in her porch till dawn. Then, still whispering, she helped him on his way. There was, of course, no one else in the house.

I made an extraordinary variety of friend-ships, many of which have lasted. One was an American bishop whom I encountered in Stewart Island, the most southerly set-tlement in New Zealand. We now have a pact never to meet in the same place twice, so we have met in Surrey, Yorkshire, Ork-ney, Des Moines (Iowa) and Timaru, New Zealand. He offered the Gulf States, but I was busy elsewhere, and he was too busy in India for me to join him. I was given sole charge of a farm in a place called The Forgotten Valley with sole responsibility for some cows, chooks and the nicest dog in the world; I had to memorise the lay of the rubber water pipes so that I could avoid treading on the resident Red-bellied Black Snake (another of the Big Ten). I was robbed of twenty NZ dollars by a teenage runaway and immediately caught up in the fascinating system of dealing with juvenile crime in an under-populated area. And I became friends with the finest swamp kauri worker in the world. Kauri trees used to dominate the northern forests of New Zealand. They are long-lived and produce the loveliest grain. 30-50,000 years ago, some fell into a Ti Tree swamp and were preserved. Ric has a licence to work this wood, and he has finally turned to wild-life sculpture. His work commands huge figures, but he charged me far less than it is worth for a prize-winning carving of a whale's tail. The gum in the wood, and the fiddleback grain, mean that the tail 'moves' like a hologram when you turn it. 'I want you to have it because you know what it is really worth' he said, not mean-ing dollars. It is one of my most precious possessions.

And what did I discover on this time of escape? That that my heart was bigger than I thought. It had not squeezed out my family or my friends, but had instead become enormously elastic, encompassing lizards and ants and snakes and fearful landscapes. I knew how the great gum trees felt when they split their bark and were suddenly relieved, and the new shiny trunk was revealed, there, ready all the time, though nobody had known.

But if you were to ask me what I value most about that time, then I would have to say that it was the discovery of the art of being present. Perhaps you know this story:

A disciple asked the Holy One:

> *Where should I look for enlightenment?*
> *Here.*
> *When will it happen?*
> *It is happening right now.*
> *Then why don't I experience it?*
> *Because you do not look.*
> *What should I look for?*
> *Nothing. Just look.*
> *At what?*
> *Anything your eyes light upon.*

Must I look in a special kind of way?

No, the ordinary way will do.

But don't I always look the ordinary way?

No, you don't.

Why ever not?

Because to look you must be here.

You're mostly somewhere else.

I can remember being in the most marvellous deserted anchorages in the Eastern Mediterranean where the kids and my husband were listening to the radio or a tape, or reading books, which had absolutely nothing to do with where we were. I have been in the most delicately honey-smelling or peat-steaming tracks with people who smoked cigarettes. I have led schoolchildren along the boardwalks of the island where I work hearing behind me a constant stream of gossip about teachers. I actually sat through a very good amateur performance of Handel's Messiah just before Christmas here in Whangaparaoa next to a woman doing Su Do Ku puzzles. I have spent the last evening of two weeks on the Isles of Scilly quite alone because everyone else was watching an episode of a classic serial on BBC 2. I felt like the odd one out for silently minding, and yes, I was the odd one out. The difference is that I no longer mind. I have ways, I find ways, of being present. Otherwise, why go?

Bird-watching and the writing of poetry have that in common – that they require you to be present. I am increasingly saddened that it is possible to take people to wonderful places and hear them say 'I saw no birds' or even 'I saw no whales'. They really are out there. We just have to look, listen, sometimes sniff. There is something you catch out of the corner of your eye, a scuttle of something in the undergrowth, a pattern of waves at sea which just looks different from the rest. The awkward, the unexpected, the surprise. But for these you have to be there.

And yes, I did come back. By then my kids had stopped judging me and were agog to know what I'd be up to next. And my husband had gone through an enormous re-assessment of who I was.

We now spend almost half the year in New Zealand where I work for the Department of Conservation, helping members of the public find rare endemic birds. And on the way there and back we go to places on the way, because everywhere is on the way. But we don't always go together now – and that is another difference. Together we have travelled Trinidad and Tobago, Sweden, Argentina and Chile. He has been to places which hold no interest for me, while I take my own trips to others. Occasionally we hit the same spots: he was in Canberra on the evening I did a poetry performance with a feisty Australian lesbian who writes material for the Sydney Opera House. He had never before heard me perform my own work and told me, surprised, 'But I thought you came out of that contest better than she did!' There are still ways, you see, that I can surprise them all.

A couple of weeks ago I was in Wellington, New Zealand's capital city, on New Year's Eve with only hours to go before sailing to the South Island. Wandering on my own I slipped into a little shop which caught my eye. Under the glass I found a heavy silver pendant – a carousel horse. The assistant told me 'It's the only one this artist has made, and she won't be making any more. It was a whim, a bit of a surprise for her. It came in today.' That's now another very precious possession.

etcetera

You gain strength, courage, and confidence by every experience in which you really stop to look fear in the face. You must do the thing which you think you cannot do.   Eleanor Roosevelt

Don't be afraid to go out on a limb. That's where the fruit is.
H Jackson Browne

I'm not afraid of storms, for I'm learning how to sail my ship.
Louisa May Alcott

You don't have to go half-way round the world to discover the joys of freedom or those challenges that bring out a new you (or the old you that may have been hiding for years). It may be easier to make big, dramatic changes in your life if you physically remove yourself from the cords that are tethering you to your current ground but that's not always possible or practical. So how can we bring excitement and challenge into our lives in a more accessible way?

'Act your shoe size – not your age' was the strap line for a recent advertising campaign (but like a lot of things – thank heavens – the memory of what it was advertising has faded). The nice thing about this quip is that it gives you choice – you can go for British (size 6 1/2) or European (38).

What IS 'age appropriate behaviour'? Should we care if our behaviour embarrasses our children? Is it their fear of our doing ourselves harm which arouses disapproval or their concern that we'll make them look foolish?

ANNOUNCEMENT

Jan Etherington

When I am an old woman, I intend to be

Sought out by the young, keen to be seen with me.

Curious and aware of life beyond my door

A stranger to ennui, a lover of Dior.

Age shall not wither me, while moisturising creams

Keep tiny lines at bay and lubricate my dreams.

Frequently in Tuscany, fabulous with flowers

Erudite and witty, closeted for hours

As confidante and friend to those who make the news;

Something of an expert on both rhythm and the blues

Marvellously funny – with an enquiring mind

Glamorous and chic – and stunning from behind.

Busy with new projects, onto the next page

It will be said about me 'She's great – for any age.'

So when I am an old woman, if I start wearing purple
and running sticks along railings . . .

Shoot me!

> After reading Jenny Joseph's poem, *Warning*
> (*When I am an old woman I shall wear purple*),
> Jan Etherington decided her attitude to growing
> older was very different . . .
>
> You can find *Warning* and other similar poems
> about ageing on www.luvzbluez.com/purple.html

A donation has been made to Jan Etherington's chosen charity ~ **The Princess Alice Hospice** is based in Esher, Surrey. They provide specialist palliative care services for patients in our catchment area, which covers South West London and most of Surrey.

They aim to control pain and other symptoms and to provide support to patients and their families according to their individual needs.

Their services are available to patients regardless of age, race or creed. They make no charge for any of their services, but rely on their own fundraising efforts and a modest NHS contribution

www.princess-alice-hospice.org.uk

GRANDMOTHERS OF THE REVOLUTION

Jean Stogdon

In essence my maternal grandmother, Catherine, born in 1877 in Wales, my mother Mary, born 1902 in Wales, and me, born 1928 in London, were all attempting to achieve the same goal as grandmothers. Despite the different social, political and emotional experiences we had, we were all first mothers and then grandmothers involved in the care of our grandchildren.

I believe that we, as grandmothers, were strong caregivers who tried (and in my case still try) to instill in our grandchildren a sense of humanity and an ability to prevail. They were role models for me, before the invention of the term – they taught me how to live and behave and care – and I attempt to be the same for my grandchildren.

The significant difference occurs because their roles were limited and more clearly defined and constrained. Both Catherine and my mother Mary were wives, mothers, grandmothers, aunts, sisters, nieces and cousins – but that is all they were or seemed to be; they had no other permitted identity beyond those familial ones. As I left school at 14 in 1942, married at 19 in 1948 and had three children in the 50s, it was perhaps natural to think that I would also be confined to those roles.

In 1966 however an event occurred which changed my life forever and led to a revolution, one that projected me out of the role of 'just a housewife'. I had a still born baby which ended prematurely my child-bearing years and forced me to look beyond the role of full-time mother. I jumped the high wall which enclosed the world of marriage and motherhood and ventured into the wider world.

While I knew I was doing something unusual in the 60s in the suburbs, where none of my friends or neighbours went out to work, I had no idea that in order to gain a separate professional identity outside the family I would have to go through so much anger and pain. Clearly in those days I had not heard of 'strategies to manage change'. I was doing the unforgivable by stepping out of my appointed role. I chose social work or rather it chose me. Of the several older women on my course all divorced soon after completing their training. That was the difference between Catherine, my mother and me; she, and her generation, never threatened the status quo or had the opportunity to do so, except by maverick, unsanctioned acts with the risk of ostracism and shame.

Catherine's life had been cruelly hard, yet my mother told me she was gentle, warm and kind. It is said that Catherine died at age 52 of hard work; certainly she had little of her life to call her own.

I was born 9 months before she died; my mother took me to see her once and I have always treasured the fact that she saw me.

In quite a primitive way I have always felt close and identified with her. I feel a thread running from her, through my mother and me to my granddaughters Hannah, Grace and Molly, although of course they have other influences too and other progenitors. I feel Catherine's influence to this day.

Catherine was born in a remote village on the Lleyn Peninsula in North Wales in 1877. It is said she was born in the same hour as her grandmother died. She married James and had three daughters followed by five sons; my mother was the second eldest daughter. James was a labourer and the family lived from hand-to-mouth. James died in 1918 aged 43. There were no widows' pensions or allowances. In that rural poverty everybody's biggest fear was the workhouse; it was a reality for many people. Catherine was fortunate enough not to live in a tied cottage when James died otherwise the family would have been evicted. As it was, James' sisters came and claimed the furniture after his death. Catherine sent my mother and one of her brothers up into the mountain with saucepans and other essentials of everyday living until the sisters had gone.

The girls in the family were sent away at age 13 to be live-in servants in the big houses in the cities; my mother went to Sheffield. The boys were sent to the big farms at the age of 12 and also lived in.

When she was 18 my mother became pregnant. This was not unusual; 'service' also had other connotations than domestic work, with the male members of the household.

For a year my mother was able to be with her daughter Mair in a mother and baby home, being a domestic, but after a year she had to leave to earn her living. She found a foster mother for Mair but on one of her visits my mother discovered they were ill treating her. She told her mother whose response was that of grandmothers through the ages when there was no alternative, she said 'bring her home, I will bring her up'. The year was 1923. Catherine had had her last child in 1915, she had been a widow for 5 years and had only six years to live. Catherine raised Mair, my half sister for 6 years until she could be reunited with her mother, when she married my father.

I became really interested in Catherine's life as I peered through the window of a 200 year old stone crog-loft cottage several years ago. This was where Catherine had been born. She was to move to a similar crog-loft cottage when she married James. How could a family of 10 people live in a single story cottage that looked like a gingerbread house with a central door and a sash window on either side? One window was in the parents' bedroom, the only bedroom and the other was the only living room. It would have had an open fire with trivets that hold a large black cast iron saucepan on one and a huge black kettle on the other. There would have been a slate floor and simple table and benches. An important piece of furniture was a 'Cwp-wrddgwydyr' (glass fronted cupboard) that held all the family's treasures; a souvenir cup brought back by a relative from a day trip to Llandudno; a birthday card, sepia with roses; a silk card sent back by a soldier from the trenches in France; and a piece of Victorian cranberry glass.

The cottage was lit by oil lamp and candles in the bedroom. On the side of the room was a tall single ladder that went up to the crog loft, there all the children, plus any visitors or lodgers, would sleep on their mattresses on the floor. According to a census there were 12 people sleeping in the cottage one night.

All the cooking would be done on the open fire. The large black saucepan would hold 'Lobscows', a sort of stew consisting of a small piece of bacon from their own pig, cabbage and potatoes. A small oven alongside, heated by the fire, would bake the 'Bara Brith', a fruit loaf for special occasions. The kettle would perpetually 'sing' ready to offer a cup of tea for any visitor who came through the ever-open door.

There would be an outside pump for water and a bucket in a small shed at the end of the garden which was the lavatory. On one side of the cottage would be a cowshed and a pigsty. The butter would be churned from the milk and sold, as were the eggs from the chickens. The residue from the butter was buttermilk which, mashed with potatoes was a staple in the family diet, and was called 'Tatwsllaith'. My mother asked for buttermilk as she was dying. As I looked through that crog loft window I longed to know about the detail of Catherine's life. What happened to her in an ordinary day? What did she wear? How did she give birth? How had she managed to raise all those children to be decent human beings against all the odds? What was James like as a husband?

I know statistically Catherine would have lost children between those that survived. I know she would have given birth at home and that birthing was 'women's business' – neighbours, friends and relatives all helping out when needed.

I knew that death was part of life. Death happened at home and was managed by families. At a recent funeral I attended in the same area there was a noticeable absence of professionals. The coffin was carried by male relatives who walked from the chapel to the cemetery.

Sex, birth, death, poverty, work and love were the elements of Catherine's life. One word describes it – survival.

My parents' home, mine until I married at 19 and theirs from 1935 until 1982 and 1985 respectively, was a small two-up-two-down Victorian terrace in New Southgate, London with an outside lavatory. A bathroom was fitted in 1968. Both my grandmother and my mother spent the best part of Monday doing the washing. If it could not be dried outside it would have been hung about wet indoors. If there was one item in my life that contributed to my liberation more than any other it was a washing machine. Although I have lived in a good three bedroomed house from 1955 to date, I did not have a washing machine until my youngest son was born in 1959. It wasn't until 1969 that I had an automatic washing machine, and that and my mother's help enabled me to combine home and work.

Both my mother and my grandmother gave birth at home. I was a 10lb baby and the birth was difficult but there were very few caesarian sections in 1928. Neither my grandmother, my mother or myself had fathers present at the births, although in 1951 when I had my first child it was beginning to happen. I had all my children in hospital with a great deal of intervention.

A most vital factor in all our lives was health. My mother told me the village barber extracted teeth and even took out tonsils; people of that class would hardly have seen a doctor. Throughout my childhood I was aware that the doctor cost 3/6p and was rarely visited. The National Health Service started in 1948, the year I married. My family has had wonderful health care for over 50 years, free of anxiety.

My mother became a housewife in 1927 when she married my father. She never worked outside the home except for a bit of 'charring'. Although I was raised during the 1930s depression my father, as a skilled engineer, was never out of work. He was a proud man, one of eight children born to Victorian parents steeped in the work ethic. His mother stayed at home and raised the children and although the number of children in families had greatly reduced in the 30s he would have thought himself a failure if his wife went out to work and usurped his role as a provider.

Therefore my mother, having brought up my sister, brother and myself moved seamlessly from her role as a full time mother to a full time grandmother when I had my first child at age 22. I had not known my grandmother as she died so young but my children knew their four grandparents into adult life. My mother's life was her children and grandchildren. She was bonded to them and they adored her. My children were deeply affected by her death at age 82. She had been a significant and important person to them.

Despite the improved physical circumstances of my mother's life, one word I believe describes her life – loss. Loss of her child Mair's early childhood, loss of another child to adoption; Catherine could not care for two grandchildren. Loss of three brothers at a young age through ill-health, loss of so many childhood friends through TB, loss of cousins killed in the

1914-1918 war, loss of her parents at so young an age. Ironically though her grand-parents lived into old age.

When I became a grandmother 19 years ago, in 1981, I was a manager of 200 staff in a very busy inner London Social services department. I worked very long hours and was almost unavailable as a child care resource for my grandchildren. I felt very guilty as my grandchildren were variously cared for in day nurseries, with child mind-ers and nannies. I questioned whether my career was more important than caring for my grandchildren whilst their parents worked. With a great struggle I came to terms with the fact, as today's parents have to, that we have choices – we live in different times.

That dilemma continues for many grand-parents to this day. We have done our bit, even the double shift; we look forward to freedom from work and to a certain extent from family responsibilities. We have responsibilities to ourselves. We have thirty odd years extra life this century and are fitter. There are greater opportunities for older people. If one word describes my life it is – choice.

If grandparents are not what they used to be neither is the task of being a grandpar-ent; we are in transition. Family life has changed so dramatically in the past dec-ade with working parents and the divorce rate so high. There is great diversity and ostensibly many options; it seems everyone wants to define and redefine family life. Grandparents are in the eye of the storm of change. Both my grandmother's and my mother's marriages were terminated by death; my own marriage is 52 years old yet already one of my sons is divorced. Divorce is a family business with grandparents witnessing the painful process but being powerless to do anything but stand by and support.

We have been lucky since having sons increases the risk of losing touch with or even being denied contact with our grand-children. Fortunately our relationship with our grandchildren is valued and continues to grow and if anything contact is even more frequent as we adopt and adapt to the role of babysitters.

There are many different issues for grand-parents depending on the circumstances of our children. Some people will become grandparents by adoption, or they may lose their grandchildren through adoption. Others will have grandchildren in lesbian or gay households and may have to come to terms with what was previously unthink-able. A few will have grandchildren subject to care proceedings because their grand-children have been neglected or abused. Furthermore, grandchildren could have at least one parent from a different ethnic group. We may lose grandchildren through divorce or gain grandchildren and become step grandparents. Our grandchildren's parents may be disabled or the children may need special help. All those situations and many others are ripe for conflict.

Taking advantage of the greater oppor-tunities for older people, at age 71 I was fortunate enough to travel to America on a Winston Churchill Fellowship to study grandparents. Four million grandparents in the USA are raising their grandchildren, parenting again when they thought they were free of full child care responsibilities for the first time.

Most grandparents will step in, as did Catherine and my mother if needs must, but there is evidence that there may be ambivalence if we are asked to do too much, at a moment when we are poised to pursue our own choices and opportunities, perhaps for the first time after a life of work.

But love is deep and family continuity and family preservation are vitally important to most grandmothers; although most of our caring is invisible and unsung I believe it is the glue that holds many families together. Stability and the extended family has never been needed more than now with the nuclear family under such stress.

A profound change – a revolution – has occurred; my grandmother and mother were its quiet and determined and even unwitting authors. I have inherited their values, and must give voice to their achievements and re-create their example for today.

etcetera

Modern older women have come to accept that their happiness and well-being depends, at least to some extent, on being able to 'do our own thing'. The role of the completely committed carer – whether through choice or circumstances – with no time to herself – is well known to be neither a happy or a healthy one. Like all things in life, striking a balance is best but balancing choice and duty can be difficult and painful. How can we do it?

Or have todays' generation of older women tasted freedom and become selfish?

Does our freedom and the activities it leads us into make it easier for us to understand and share things with the younger generation? It is said that understanding often skips a generation.

How important is it to have a significant 'label'? Did/does the confidence of the woman who 'doesn't work outside the home' suffer from the lack of an accepted 'label'? Does it help to be able to call yourself a 'homemaker' (or some such phrase) as opposed to that apologetic response when asked 'What do you do?' – 'Oh, I don't do anything' or 'I'm just a housewife'?

DEFINING WOMEN

TURTLE ISLAND

Maggie Guillon

Every inch of her clothing stuck to her body like hot plastic. The hand that supported her on her dusty stick throbbed with blisters, and with each step powdered earth rose in small clouds and bonded to her legs in patterns of perspiration. The rest of the group had opted for a brisk march up the beach to see Monitor lizards and, knowing that she wouldn't keep up

in the sizzling humidity, Alice had chosen instead to explore the small fishing village that rested against the shore like a pack of cards. For some inexplicable reason she wanted to wander among the houses - bamboo shacks on stilts - and just be alone for a while.

Her aloneness was a cruel one here. Bony children ran behind her sniggering, scampering off into the blousy vegetation when she turned her head. Shadowy shapes moved under each house and beneath one of them she could dimly make out a hammock swinging over a cluster of scavenging roosters. The heat was stifling, and her head spun with the overhead cacophony of insects and birds. Every so often she recoiled slightly from the heavy odour of fish and sewerage.

In the muted space beneath the largest of the houses lay a row of boats in various stages of completion, their white wood skeletons ethereal against the dusty floor. Squatting amongst them was a scrawny fisherman hacking away at a plank with a large machete. He was naked except for a pair of shabby shorts and a sprinkling of fine yellow wood chippings. Alice raised her camera for a moment then thought better of it. She was unsure how little brown people felt about image taking, and was especially wary of those wielding machetes. With clumsy, arthritic poise she moved slowly across his light and back to the path.

He glanced up and watched her for a moment. She looked enormous against the brightness of the midday sun. Who was this creature with black sunshade holes for eyes, whose big white body oozed and dripped with every sweltering step? What did she want? Her face was turned towards him but hidden below the shadow of a large sunhat – they come here seeking light, he muttered, but bring their own darkness with them. He drew tightly on his cigarette stub and turned back to the rhythmic thwack-thwack of blade into wood, one eye still following the intruder.

As her passing brushed against the solid air, three staccato bottlebrush chick heads poked out through the slats of a small raised hut. Their plaintive chirrup stirred a twinge of English sentimentality and she glanced away as an emaciated, scabby dog loped across her path and dropped under the hut into the pretence of shade. It sniffed listlessly at a tiny dark shape in the dust and she paused - a spider, snake? No, a tiny turtle hatchling trapped between two large pots. It must have emerged sometime in the night and become disorientated on its way from nest to ocean. Perhaps it had spent hours there scrabbling feebly against the cold stone in its blind compulsion to find the sea.

Unaware that she was still being observed, she lifted the fragile shell between thumb and forefinger and placed it in one hand,

closing the other over it like a cocoon, soothing it between her sweaty palms. Leaving her stick where it lay in the dusty earth, she moved slowly out between the huts and onto the sand. It was gritty with fragments of dead coral that flamed against her calloused feet. But she kept walking with a blind compulsion of her own.

He watched her moving along the waterline, this way, that way, until she reached the perfect spot and placed the hatchling gently into a dappled wave. He watched as she straightened awkwardly. He watched the shadow of her spirit swimming out alongside in a graceful, protective curve until the tiny struggling creature was lost from view.

Alice stood there for a long, long time. Eventually the fisherman laid his machete to one side and walked down to the beach carrying a small bowl of cool brown water for the strange white woman with no eyes.

etcetera

Does life experience make it easier to build bridges between cultures, or do we become more set in our ways and therefore less amenable to difference?

Are our innermost yearnings universal?

WHY WOMEN DON'T RELAX

Germaine Greer

Women either don't do leisure, or they do free leisure, or at best cheap leisure, or they fail to perceive any difference between work and leisure. Ask what a woman's leisure activity is and you're apt to be told, 'Shopping.' Shopping is grinding toil that women mistake for play. Men stand bemused as women trudge from shop to shop looking for something better or cheaper than another thing that is virtually identical, wondering why they didn't buy what they wanted at the first shop that had it in stock. Men don't understand that if you haven't come close to dropping, then you haven't shopped. Men buy; women shop.

Most women would say that they have very little time to themselves. The time they don't spend working for the employer and the taxman they spend doing something called 'housework', to which, for most women between the ages of 25 and 50, may be added 'childcare'. There is also the onerous task of body maintenance, keeping the otherwise disgusting female body clean, tidy, deodorised, made up, not to mention toned and becomingly clad, plus the exhausting, sometimes painful and expensive business of hair and hairiness management. Work, all of it.

There are powerful historical reasons for women's imperviousness to the demands of leisure. The typical world citizen – who is still female, illiterate and an unpaid family worker – knows only too well that if she is ever to be seen with her hands in her lap, a job will be found for her. In traditional societies, the high days and holidays on which menfolk are permitted to straighten their backs and put on clean clothes are the days on which the women have to work the hardest, smartening up the house and putting together giant meals. It is not so long ago that on Sundays, while rest of the family frolicked, the woman of the house had to cook and serve a three-course Sunday lunch and clean up after it.

Many women these days would like nothing better than the chance to serve soup, roast and pudding to the assembled family once a week. If they don't do it any more, it is less because they rebelled against such hard labour on everybody else's day of rest than because nowadays there isn't anybody around to eat the food they cook. Everybody else is out doing leisure. Has the woman of the house grabbed a kitbag and followed their example? Apparently not. Women don't go fishing. Women do play golf, but not many and not much. Women don't buy sports equipment or season tickets. Women don't buy sports cars, boats, jetskis, trailbikes, guns, crossbows . . . Women don't collect stamps, spot trains, buy music products. Women do use gyms, but not for fun.

If leisure is what you do when you are not working for a livelihood, then the women who were excluded from the paid workforce never had anything but leisure, but their leisure, as Thorstein Veblen explained, was vicarious leisure, its purpose to display for all to see the status of the man who owned them and could afford to let them sit about all day every day. Ladies of leisure were not permitted to enjoy their leisure. They couldn't go rambling about or fishing or playing cricket on the green or burying themselves in books. Instead, they had to fill their hours with useless, pointless, unproductive, repetitive work: beadwork, shellwork, tatting, making cut-paper patterns and silhouettes, japanning, plus what

George Eliot called 'a little ladylike tinkling and smearing'. For the affluent, housework used to be done by servants. Boiling up shirts and sheets, ironing, polishing floors and furniture, blacking grates and shining silver used to be heavy work. The lady of the middle-class house wasn't expected to break into a sweat. It was only when machines replaced maids that vicarious leisure could take the form of housework.

Occasionally some foolhardy academic tries to suggest that housework is a leisure pursuit, the paradigmatic 'leisure industry', which is one way of saying 'keeping very busy doing nothing'. Women will not accept this version of their reality; they want us to believe that they hate and resent housework, but that 'someone has to do it'. The people who make money out of this kind of leisure industry are multinationals like Unilever and Procter & Gamble, and by manipulating women's insecurities they make unimaginably huge amounts of it. Currently, women are fighting a war on bacteria, nasty, deformed aliens who hide under toilet seats and on work surfaces. Where lazy boys play murderous videogames, diligent housewives deal out death and destruction to an equally fictitious enemy. The boys know they are playing; the women think they are working.

The men's leisure industry covets the trillions of dollars' profit made by Unilever and Procter & Gamble. If it has seriously tried to entice women away from the housework and win back the money they splurge on home-care, there is no sign of its succeeding. Half of the population remains inaccessible to the leisure industry because of the fantasy war against filth, which requires the cleaning of a house already too clean. I have yet to see any ad appearing in a women's magazine saying, 'Your house is clean enough. Come out and play!' In a current women's magazine, one advertisement shows a bare-chested hunk on a sunset beach holding what appears at first glance to be a boogie board. In fact it is an ironing board, and the advertisement challenges its readers, 'Still finding excuses to keep your old ironing board?' The same magazine carries two advertisements for cars, one of which begins, 'Slip behind the wheel of a new Ford Territory and you can relax in the knowledge that you're surrounded by a legion of safety features' – and proceeds to list them all. No suggestion that driving a car might be fun, in fact, nothing about the car's performance at all.

Women are not listening to the siren call of leisure. But it is also true that the leisure industry does not address itself to women. This may be simply because no female market exists, but an elderly market certainly exists and the leisure industry ignores that too, even though older people have more disposable income than younger people. The goods and services older people use are never characterised as such. The explanation is not simply that advertisers are ageist, but that senior citizens themselves are ageist. The greyest of nomads would not buy an RV that was advertised as ideal for grey nomads.

Older women, whether they play bingo or break out the camp stove, are heavily involved in leisure, but theirs is cut-price leisure. They are not in the market for recreational vehicles, or powerboats, or even motel accommodation. They are the people who make possible literary festivals and antique fairs, who support local art galleries and museums, who volunteer for every community chore, and happily raise money for what they believe to be good causes, giving, giving, giving of their time free. If we had a way of quantifying the output of the leisure industry of older women, we would probably see that it contributes vastly more to the GDP than the corporate leisure industry.

This article is published here by the kind permission of Germaine Greer. It was originally published in *The Guardian* on Thursday May 4, 2006 and follows from Professor Greer's speech at Permira Leisureland, a panel debate on the future of the leisure industry in the UK.

A donation has been made to Germaine Greer's chosen charity ~
Buglife - The Invertebrate Conservation Trust is the first
organisation in Europe devoted to the conservation of all invertebrates.
It is actively engaged in saving Britain's rarest bugs, slugs, snails, bees,
wasps, ants, spiders, beetles and many more fascinating invertebrates
by:

- Undertaking and promoting crucial study and research

- Promoting sound management of land and water to maintain and
  enhance invertebrate biodiversity

- Supporting the conservation work of other entomological and
  conservation organisations

- Promoting education and publicising invertebrates and their
  conservation, and influencing invertebrate conservation in Europe
  and worldwide.

Buglife The Invertebrate Conservation Trust
170A Park Road
Peterborough   PE1 2UF
info@buglife.org.uk
www.buglife.org.uk
01733 201 210

MY NEWEST CAREER

astra

How many nations consider their small children worthy of high salaried, high status carers? I'm talking about nursery and creche staff, child minders and, of course, mothers. Such is the low esteem in which our society holds its children that, years ago, when I retired, I began earning more per hour as a domestic cleaner that I ever did as an under-fives community play leader (working for three different local government authorities in London) or, more recently, as a nanny. I suspect that similar conditions exist elsewhere in Europe and the rest of the 'developed' world.

In any event, as a retired woman I needed all the cash I could earn. My state pension is pathetic (the lowest in Europe bar Greece) and not a full one at that. Any job-related superannuation wasn't available because I had been a part-time employee (like an enormous number of women of all ages). Lodgers, to supplement my income, were and still are, in short supply. So are the poetry readings and workshops I used to do. My financial situation is far from exceptional, especially among younger women; we are generally regarded as burdens and nuisances in any industrialised culture. And money is a taboo subject, or rather the absence of it; we mustn't admit to being poor (in middle class circles anyway, where it's viewed as personal failure).

So . . . I've found cleaning, tidying and organising someone else's territory much less stressful than child care (despite having been stimulated and delighted by this activity, both paid and unpaid, in the distant past). And because the results of organising, tidying and cleaning some-one else's space were immediate, I found it gratifying work: washing up, wiping shelves, mopping and sweeping floors, hoovering, sorting cupboards, desks, draw-ers and wardrobes, changing bed linen, dusting books and bric-a-brac, cleaning toilets, ovens, fridges, windows and sinks, folding towels and sheets, hanging up clothes, polishing mirrors and the family silver, emptying ashtrays, carrying out the rubbish etc etc – all took on a new lustre: it must have been the lucre. Of course, wives and mothers, sisters and daughters the world over do all this and more all of the time, all of their lives. But they're accorded status (sometimes) in lieu of payment. Frankly, I'd rather have the money. (By the way, I called my one woman service 'Order Out of Chaos').

Observing the reactions among some of my friends when I told them I'd become a cleaner mirrored my own inner disquiet and dismay, at least at first. They too were surprised, even shocked. But I'm keenly aware that purist and class-based attitudes towards certain kinds of work, especially labour that soils the hands, pay no bills. Manual workers are scorned in many parts of the world and cleaners are no exception. Over time my friends grew accustomed to my newest career and so did I.

Many of us have needed to do casual, that is, untaxed, work throughout our lives. So have our mums and grannies. But radical analyses, eg. feminism and Marxism, require flexible, practical responses. After all, few of us have private incomes or generous partners or high salaried, secure careers. Historically, housekeeping as paid employment, has been one of a limited range of job possibilities available to women, especially as we age. UK Equal Opportunity policies regarding age, gender etc aren't being consistently enforced. Thus individual cleaning jobs are open to exploitation as long as there are no legally binding job descriptions and conditions of employment, ie. trade union contracts or central government statutes.

But it is the contradiction inherent in my newest career that angers me: cleanliness receiving higher remuneration than nurturing (of the young, the elderly, the disabled etc); house servants/domestics being paid more (in most cases) than carers.

Hypocrisy lives, alas.

etcetera

What impact does a label – pinned on us because of how we make a living – have on who we really are or how we see ourselves? Surely it's all about our attitude to the job. If we see the job as demeaning then we will be demeaned by it. If we see it as simply a means to an end then we maintain our integrity. (Or could that be taken too far – does morality come into it?)

It may work the other way (from astra's experience). A highly paid lawyer, for instance, may be looked up to because of her position but, in reality, may not be worthy of that respect. Stereotypes linked to 'what we do' are invariably reinforced by society and the media and, all too often, used as shorthand to dictate assumptions about individuals.

Is there any relationship between what people earn and their 'value' to humanity? If we assumed that most people agree that caring for children and other vulnerable people is deemed to be important to society as a whole how would we place various jobs and professions on a list of highest to lowest salaries?

DEFINING WOMEN

OBSERVATIONS:
A LIGHT-HEARTED LOOK AT LIFE

Jessie Coning

Jessie Coning has, for years, taught a yoga class that ended with a discussion session. What follows is a distillation from the many pieces she has written to read out to the women in the group in order to get the conversation flowing.

THE MELODRAMA
[*'A play full of suspense in a sensational and emotional style'*]

When my husband had a stroke, my life suddenly changed overnight from one of comfortable routine. There were ups and downs, of course, but nothing that I couldn't handle. My life became a 'melo-drama'. When someone asked me how things were at home – I saw a green light to launch into all the depressing details. Our trouble is that no one else out there had such troubles as we have!

A wise teacher once said something that helped me to think differently about my personal melodrama: 'Of course life is not fair. It was never intended to be. No one ever said that it was – but life is like school – and each one of us privileged to be living on this beautiful earth at this time is here to learn lessons'. Learning lessons can become quite an interesting occupa-tion – it certainly slows down the growing old process.

When you and I are going through one of our own personal dramas, we do get things out of proportion. Life is not really so bad as we are making it out to be.

I'm sure we have all watched one of the TV soaps and noticed how the characters take little things so seriously – 'How can this be happening to me', they react. Then they exacerbate the problem by telling everyone 'how awful' it is!

I still find myself getting dramatic on occa-sions – especially if I have a sympathetic listener close at hand – but now, I usually remember to say to myself, 'Whoops, here I go again – starting my own personal soap opera'. This nearly always takes the edge off my seriousness and helps me laugh at myself and soon my patient listener is laughing with me.

LISTENING
There is a big difference between hearing and listening. When I sit on the bench at the top of the garden with my morning coffee – I can hear the distant traffic roll-ing along but if there is a breeze stirring the leaves of the big old tree nearby – that is what I am listening to. On one of these occasions I closed my eyes and could begin to understand why people say they would choose (if they had a choice) to lose their sight rather than their sense of hearing.

What would it be like not to be able to hear the voices of those we love, or the waves crashing against the shore or a chuckle of a baby.

TODAY IS ALL WE HAVE

A student of philosophy wandered into a hallway one day impatiently wondering when his lesson would begin and noticed a mop and broom. Actually the mop and broom had been left there for the student to notice. The lesson had already begun. Do what is in front of you and don't worry about what more 'important' lessons may need to be learned in the future – until you have swept clean the hallway that leads you there.

Here's a personal example: life is moving along comfortably – I have a nice home, enough money for my needs and a little spare for a holiday or a new coat. My husband has a retirement job and interests outside the home. I, likewise, am free to follow my chosen lifestyle.

Overnight he is struck down with a life-threatening illness and my life collapses. I am thrown into the role of carer and I bitterly resent the stealing away of my freedom. I resent my home being turned upside down to accommodate the needs of the patient. My heart and blood pressure moves to dangerous levels – another problem to be resolved. The prospect of this situation continuing for years or even months is intolerable. But I slowly begin to realise that the only way to overcome the catastrophe is to live one day at a time.

I will do what lies in front of me today. I will take up my 'mop and broom'. I will prepare a nourishing meal and serve it with a fresh napkin and a smile. I will meet petulance with patience and when the evening comes my halo may have slipped a little – and I will have lost my cool once or twice and taken a few short cuts in the cleaning, but I will have put a little time aside just for me – a time to rest with my feet up and time for an hour with a friend or for a little outing.

All this dedication doesn't mean I have to settle for this kind of life for the rest of my days – but taking up my daily challenge that is right there in front of me – without becoming a victim of it, helps me to grow mentally and spiritually and when the mental attitude is right, bodily health begins to improve.

LITTLE LESSONS CAN MAKE A BIG DIFFERENCE

Over the years (as a Yoga Stress Relief Tutor) I've discovered that as we teach others we are also students – learning all the time. I've learned that the best way to release an emotional problem is to talk to someone – I don't mean making a pest of ourselves by whining and complaining – but decide on someone we can trust and ask them for their advice. Tell them you have a problem and you'd like them to listen. They may see angles that you can't but even if they can't it will help you a lot if they just listen while you talk it out.

It is also helpful to keep a special notebook for inspirational reading (what people used to call a 'Commonplace Book'). Into this you can paste or write poems, prayers and quotations which appeal to you personally and which give you a lift. Reading through it is like a spiritual shot in the arm.

I have learned not to dwell too long on the shortcomings of others – particularly after overhearing a woman in a café say 'Oh yes, like yours, my husband has many faults . . . if he had been a saint he never would have married me'.

"Accentuate the positive – eliminate the negative. Latch on to the affirmative – don't mess with Mr In Between."

Several ladies in my class said they felt driven and harassed by unending housework and things that they simply had to do every day. I suggested that if they drew up a schedule each night for the following day – more work would be accomplished with less fatigue, a feeling of achievement and there would be time left to rest and pamper themselves. By structuring your time you will feel in control of your life.

And finally – if we are going to make things better for others, let's be quick about it. I shall pass this way but once, therefore any good that I can do or kindness that I can show – let me do it now.

THINKING POSITIVELY

I have two friends who, like me, have health problems but always seem happy and relaxed. They say they believe in positive thinking. There's no magic wand but here's what you can do.

Begin by speaking only happy and positive words when you hold a conversation. Try to stop yourself from saying things like 'I'm always doing stupid things – opening my mouth and putting my foot in it' or 'That horse won't come first with my luck'. By thinking that way you draw trouble to you.

Try and change your circumstances by starting to think differently. I'll let you in on a secret. If you think unhappy thoughts you will be unhappy, no matter what's going on around you. Instead of looking out at the world and thinking of it as a dangerous place full of drugs, drop-outs and rapists – see it as a friendly place. You know there are lots of lovely, friendly people out there. Concentrate on them and on the beautiful world with its lakes and mountains and glorious sunsets. 'Two men looked out of the same prison bars – one saw mud and the other saw the stars.'

Practice politeness in your conversation – not for the benefit of others but for your own wellbeing. You will draw others to you – they will like being around you.

Let the other person in the conversation be right – this doesn't necessarily mean that you are wrong. When someone says 'I'm too old to change' they are deluding themselves and simply being negative. Avoid needless arguments – the force of energy wasted is enormous. Negative energy destroys relationships, but most importantly it weakens you.

No one can be positive all the time. When a negative sentence pops out (and it will because we are not perfect) you will hear yourself saying it and it will bring a smile to your lips.

RANDOM ACTS OF KINDNESS

Does the routine of our daily lives mean we have little time for random thoughts or acts of kindness – acts that would brighten someone else's day and contribute to our own health and wellbeing?

A friend from America reported how some drivers started paying the toll of the car behind them on the Golden Gate Bridge. You would drive up, brandish your dollar or whatever only to be told 'Your toll has been paid by the car ahead of you'. You can imagine the impact that such a small gift had on the driver. Maybe it encouraged him to be nicer person for the rest of the day. A single act of kindness can set a ripple of kind acts in motion.

Have you ever noticed how little eye contact most of us have with strangers? I sometimes wonder why? I believe there is a connection between our attitudes towards strangers and our own level of happiness. In other words, you don't usually find that a person who walks around with their head down, frowning and looking away from people is secretly a peaceful, joyful person. The two things just don't go together!

I am not suggesting we go around grinning at everyone nor suggesting we pretend to be friendly. Maybe we could think of strangers as being a bit like ourselves and treat them not only with kindness and respect but with smiles and eye contact as well. I'll let you in on a secret – you will probably begin to notice some pretty nice changes in yourself too. So maybe the next time you come across a stranger – look them in the eye – smile – and see what happens.

COLOUR IN MY LIFE

We can go through our lives without ever giving a second thought to the effect of colour in our life. Patients in a mental hospital became calmer when the walls were changed from brown to pink. The child of a friend had his bedroom painted and papered in bright red, blue and yellow. The child was a very restless sleeper until his grandmother suggested that a pale blue or green had calming effect on the human personality. The colour scheme was changed and the child slept well!

Are we surprised when the little old lady in the pew in front of us who is always dressed all in brown is very introverted and sinks her head into her shoulders with a nervous smile if anyone tries to speak to her?

Buddhists have always worn saffron coloured robes – a deep orange that denotes the quality of wisdom. In the UK an experiment was done by placing an orange coloured sheet of paper under an exam test paper used by students. It appeared to gently stimulate the mind and improve the exam results.

Lavender (the scent, that is) is well known for its calming effect. Place a few drops of Lavender essential oil on a pinch of cotton wool and breathe deeply. In your imagination be aware of a field of lavender – row after row of this beautiful colour.

Every colour has a personality which evokes an emotional response. However, this varies from culture to culture and person to person. In the west we tend to associate black with death while in Korea the colour of death is yellow.

People wear colours that they feel suit their person or circumstances. Some older women, in particular, might think it 'unseemly' to dress brightly but others love vibrant colours and this reflects their character but do you think people can change themselves by changing their clothes?

DO YOU DRIVE YOURSELF AS WELL AS YOU DRIVE YOUR CAR?

The body and the human brain together make a very beautiful machine which is designed to last for a long time and to give its inhabitant an efficient 'working' life of 70, 80 or more years. To have a body that is smooth running it has to be extended. It needs challenges. It needs rest and rewards. This beautiful body of ours is rather like a car. What would happen if we drove our car at full throttle without any respite? It would soon end up in the garage for repairs. So why do we take so long to get the message? Life (and staying alive) is always a matter of balance – balance between activity and rest and between work and play.

Physical reactions take place when our bodies are alerted for activity – just as they did when a caveman saw a predatory animal. His body came into a 'fight or flight' state. Our caveman listened, naturally, to his inner promptings. When the threat was dealt with relaxation could and should take over. Nowadays many people tend to push themselves both physically and mentally beyond that point where we should 'switch off'.

Sages of old were right when they preached the value of the virtues of acceptance, compassion and turning the other cheek. This is not so easy to do in a competitive world but it is worth reminding yourself that 'When I get angry the only person I hurt is myself'.

When we drive we save the 'revs' for sudden speed in emergencies, hill climbing and overtaking. Let us keep our bodily revs for emergencies, 'fight or flight' situations and extreme excitement and pleasure. This way we'll keep to a minimum the wear and tear on our engines, the strain on our bodywork and the noise and discomfort to ourselves and others.

Happy journeying!

etcetera

Milton writes, in *Paradise Lost* ~ '*The mind is its own place, and in itself, can make a heaven of hell, a hell of heaven*'. As in Buddhism/meditation, there is more basis for such an approach than we realise. Modern neuroscience is now demonstrating how persistent, positive thinking actually retrains the brain, even creating new cell growth and setting new physiological patterns that can fundamentally alter the temperament. So what appear to be trite, airy-fairy platitudes can actually point us towards fascinating scientific wisdom which can assist us in taking control of biological processes.

It has been said that we do old people a disservice by not arguing with them when they make statements that we think are ridiculous or wrong. A vigorous argument is good for the brain . . . or is it 'disrespectful' to challenge the 'wisdom' of old people (as someone recently claimed on the radio)?

Can you write an episode of 'soap opera' out of something that has happened to you?

If you had to choose to lose either your sight or your hearing – which would you choose and why?

How does colour affect your mood or reflect character?

If you had to describe yourself as a particular model of car, which would it be?

ANGELA'S JUST 70 CHALLENGE

Angela Glendenning

Where to begin unless at the beginning? But where was that? I was moving towards my eighth decade. Something to mark the occasion seemed demanded. Why was that? Hadn't previous decades past relatively unremarked? They had but not my sixth decade when I was approaching 50. I recall earnestly engaging in a life review to determine where my future priorities lay. I did not want to look back later to discover my memories were laced with regrets or remorse.

Whatever my good resolutions, they quickly faded except for one. I had intimations of middle age spread! Belts were becoming tighter. It could only get worse without drastic action.

That was the 1980s and the height of the Marathon running boom. My tennis game was becoming increasingly erratic to the point of embarrassment. My husband Frank bought me a track suit and not quite knowing what to do with it I started running round the block. It was a small step to enter a Fun Run and a slightly bigger one to join a local athletic club advertising for new members. I began to be a little more adventurous. I entered a club 10k race but I hyper-ventilated on the second lap and barely finished. At the age of 48 some might think this signalled the demise of my entry into athletics, but I went down

to the club the following Wednesday and discovered that I had won an age group prize. I was hooked!

More than 20 years on I'm still running. I am not a natural runner. I discovered no hidden depth of talent or stamina. But I do have determination. Before long I began to feel fitter and to enjoyed the discipline and structure of regular training. I may not have often enjoyed a runner's 'high' but I did relish being out in all weathers and taking part in cross country. It felt like playtime all over again, splashing through the mud, sometimes in driving rain, on cold, frosty mornings wearing shorts or late on a winter's afternoon with the light fading.

Running marathons enabled me to gain a more personal entry into the culture of the prison culture where I worked as a Senior Probation Officer. Running gave me an identity that the prison officers would relate to. As a woman in a man's world running offered me a common ground – an interest in sport. More important, perhaps, I decided to raise money for The Swallows Disabled Sports Club. Each week, selected prisoners went out of the prison to assist the club. For a while some women prisoners joined from a nearby women's prison. When I announced that I was collecting sponsors for my first marathon, prisoners rallied round and their contribution and that of prison officers, colleagues and friends meant I was able to swell the coffers of The Swallows by over £1000, a goodly sum in those days.

When I started entering races, Frank was my loyal 'bagman'. No-one could have been a more committed supporter but as I became more familiar with the world of road runners and joined the North Staffs Road Runners' Association, Frank gradually withdrew. He had more profitable things to do than wait for me to complete a half marathon!

I retired in 1995, by which time Frank had already embarked on what was effectively his third career – pursuing his interests in education and ageing on both national and international scenes. For many years I had been involved with a housing association, a council for racial equality and shortly added a healthcare trust to that list. So while I worked in one room and went out to meetings, Frank worked in another – and went out to meetings! We went to Greece every spring and to other countries at other times. Frank lectured in Australia and Canada and attended various international meetings. I took time out to go to Syria and Yemen. We enjoyed the theatre and our lives were in harmony.

Gradually, the North Staffs Racial Equality Council took more and more of my time and the work wasn't always comfortable. On a number of occasions I asked myself why, when I was retired, I subjected myself to so much stress? For awhile the organisation was in melt-down. However, like running, the pain had its own reward. My life was enriched by getting to know so many people from ethnic minorities and in due course the NSREC was back on course.

BECOMING A FULL-TIME CARER

Frank died in December 2002. He was poorly for quite a long time and during his last year he was considerably incapacitated. We both remained as fully engaged in our interests and in our local community as Frank's circumstances allowed but imperceptibly I became a full-time carer. Frank, being the man he was, continued to support me in keeping a skeleton of activities going. I attended meetings, contributed what I could, and maintained a regular running routine. During Frank's last year this entailed getting up at 6.00 am and running around three miles before two carers arrived to help us start the day! I don't recollect finding it especially hard and I think regular exercise enabled me to be a better carer.

I had as much opportunity as anyone to prepare myself for Frank's dying. My mother had lingered but when she died, I was totally unprepared. She was in her 90s and I should have known but I needed someone to point out the obvious. I was determined that it would not be the same with Frank. But some lessons we don't learn. It was self evident Frank was dying but somehow I managed to sideline this knowledge. I was so prepared and yet so unprepared.

After Frank died, I felt that people had an expectation of how, as a bereaved person, I should behave. I felt as if everything with which I was involved had turned to dust and ashes – organisations with which I was involved could do without me. I felt uncertain about how to conduct myself so I fell back on advice Frank had offered years before – 'Surely you don't need to enjoy your work in the community. It's a social obligation'. I carried on and, of course, a sense of enjoyment and satisfaction returned.

It was natural, therefore, to plod on engaging in my usual interests and activities even though I had little taste for them. I felt that my life lacked focus and direction. I was at odds with myself. I believed that I needed to plough a new furrow but I didn't know how or where. I believed I should be engaging in more obvious recreational and leisure pursuits and, indeed, I tried to do so. I went on outings. I sought refuge visiting friends in France, travelling for the first time by Eurostar. I went to Lesvos for a week only to find time hanging heavy, especially in the evenings when dinner at a table by the sea lost its attraction with no-one to share it. It was a strange year.

I read about the Stroke Association's Thames Bridges Cycle Ride which struck a spark in me as Frank had suffered from strokes. I could borrow a bike and take part. The ride involved starting at Tower Bridge and cycling over 14 bridges finishing at Hampton Court.

Getting on a bike for the first time in 59 years wasn't as easy as I had expected. I hadn't bargained on the traffic. By the time I had assembled myself to move off from green traffic lights, they had turned back to red and I hadn't moved. Roundabouts were an unbelievable hazard which often involved dismounting and walking!

About the same time I went on my first full day walk with local ramblers. I was not worried about going up Kinder Scout but I was anxious about the coming down. Believing I saw our leader jump from boulder to boulder I followed suit. The moral of this story is 'don't think you know better than your leader'! I fell around 10 feet onto grit stone! Lying wedged between rocks I felt deeply embarrassed. There was blood everywhere and my fellow walkers were fearful that I had badly injured myself although I tried to reassure them. After

40 minutes the Air Ambulance and Mountain Rescue arrived and I was air lifted to hospital with a broken arm, a battered face and severe bruising. The care and support I received from colleagues and friends was enormously rewarding. What could have been a disastrous experience became one from which I drew sustenance and strength put paid to the Thames Bridges Cycle Ride.

Looking back, recovering from the accident and coping with only one arm for a number of weeks totally pre-occupied me during that summer. I did not have to think about what I would do today or tomorrow. I merely had to concentrate on managing day by day. I couldn't drive but as soon as possible I walked everywhere. On one occasion I was walking into town and a woman stopped in front of me. Looking me up and down, she declared 'You've not been dancing on the tables again'. This became my standard response when people asked what I had done to myself! The accident offered respite and a period of enforced psychological and emotional recuperation from my bereavement.

DONATING AN ORGAN

It must have been sometime during the year following Frank's death that my niece Sarah phoned and announced, 'I'm going to need a kidney transplant.' Sarah suffers from Lupus disease. This is a beastly rheumatic disease where something goes wrong with the immune system which normally protects the body against harmful agents and, due to a case of 'mistaken identity, an immune attack is mounted against the body's own tissues. For Sarah, her kidneys had come under attack. Without hesitation, I replied, 'You can have one of mine any time'.

If my broken arm had, in a manner of speaking, helped to tide me over my first year without Frank, traipsing up and down to a London hospital for blood tests, a CT scan, an ECG, renal ultrasound and more blood tests, tided me over the second year without him. By the end of the year, Sarah and I knew that the transplant operation would take place early in 2004. Thus it was that I found myself for the first time in the role of patient and, never having been on the receiving end of hospital care, I found it all an extraordinarily interesting experience.

Ninety-six to 98% of kidneys in living donor transplants are still functioning well after a year and these figures are improving all the time. Since the operation I have met countless people who have lived for many years with a transplanted kidney. Sarah and I and our family had every expectation that my donation would give Sarah a new lease of life but it was not to be. After struggling for five days to retrieve what proved to be an irretrievable situation, my kidney was removed and Sarah was back on dialysis.

For me, I can honestly say that the operation was no big deal. I felt ill for three or four days but there was always light at the end of a very short tunnel. Mine was a finite experience. Six or seven weeks after the operation I could enjoy a decent walk of five or six miles although a return to running proved harder. After a mile I found myself grinding to a halt and although I can now manage four to five miles, running remains something of a struggle.

DEFINING WOMEN

FINDING A WAY FORWARD

I returned home following the failed transplant operation, not knowing how to make sense of our experience. Obviously I had to recuperate and, of course, life goes on regardless of setbacks and what it might throw at us. I was in North Staffordshire. Sarah was in London. I was not confronted daily by what she and her family were going through. I began to learn more about the needs of transplant patients locally and to meet people who had received donated organs or were waiting for one.

I was approaching 70 and I had become aware that this might be a difficult milestone to negotiate unless, as I had done when I was approaching 50, I marked the occasion in some way. It was a small step to realize I had to claw back the initiative from our failed transplant operation. This was when *Angela's Just 70 Challenge* was born.

I decided to raise money for our two local renal and transplant patient associations, promote the NHS Organ Donor Register and to purchase a kidney dialysis machine for the Salma Dialysis Centre in Khartoum as a symbolic way of expressing my gratitude to a Sudanese doctor, Khalid Ali, now a stroke consultant, who tended Frank on one of his admissions to hospital and who cared for me after Frank died. My target was £28,000.

The strategy seemed obvious to me – I would set myself seven challenges. I would run 7 miles, walk 70 miles, swim a mile, cycle 70 miles, climb 7 tors, canoe 7 miles and horse-ride 7 miles, all within seven weeks starting with the Newcastle 7 Road Race on 3 April, 2005.

PREPARATION

First I compiled a mailing list of people and companies I could approach for support, including a local design company and a printer who would produced a promotional leaflet.

Testing my fitness in a five-mile road race I severely strained my hamstring. I thought a bit of rest would do the trick. I rested. I caught coughs and colds. I felt debilitated. I cycled a bit. I had some riding lessons. My overall fitness did not improve and I wondered why I had not thought of some fallback challenges in case I failed on one I had set myself. This was when I discovered bog snorkelling or wing walking! Meanwhile the day for my first challenge loomed closer.

Even with excellent physiotherapy I harboured serious doubts about completing my first challenge, a seven mile road race. Accompanied by two local runners, I was determined to finish even if it meant walking. Then, with the end in sight I thought I might even be enjoying it! Now it was just a question of fulfilling a challenge a week for the next six weeks.

I'M UNDERWAY

The swim (supported by friends) was straightforward. Then I went to Devon to climb seven tors with an old school friend, Sally. We were accompanied by a group of Samaritans with whom Sally has worked for many years. In her mid-sixties Sally had already raised over £10,000 for the Samaritans by walking from John o'Groats to Landsend and was also undertaking some challenges to celebrate her 70th birthday so we canoed together for seven miles on the Exeter canal. On the day we climbed the seven tors it was fine and sunny in London and Paula Radcliffe was winning the London Marathon. On Dartmoor, rain and mist descended and rapidly this became heavy rain. We often couldn't see the tors, let alone climb them. We climbed two and walked around the rest!

Sally came up to Staffordshire to join me for a 70 mile cycle ride on the Cheshire Cycleway. The weather was blustery, sunny and again wet! My new bike, donated by Raleigh, proved to be a godsend. I felt more secure and my confidence grew with each mile.

Walking 70 miles of the Staffordshire Way was, when the time came, straightforward. For the first two sections, myself and four friends joined forces with the Staffordshire Wildlife Trust who were ferrying walkers to and fro along three sections of the Way. We were given a warm reception at Abbots Bromley School for Girls at the end of the third day. The school was using my *Just 70* exhibition as an opportunity to promote the NHS Organ Donor Register as well as raising money to support my fund-raising, and members of the National Women's Register turned out to greet us. A cheque was duly presented and pictures were taken for a local newspaper.

The horse-riding definitely had the greatest WOW factor! I had a lead car, with a flashing light in front to warn pedestrians and cars that I was coming. Another rider accompanied me and two walkers kept pace behind as best they could. I would like to continue riding but there comes a point when discretion is the better part of valour. I might feel secure enough but my horse might be spooked by the unexpected and then there is no knowing what the outcome might be.

BOG SNORKELLING AND WING WALKING

My 'reserve events', the World Bog Snorkelling Championships at Llanwrtyd Wells in Wales and the Wing Walk at Rendcomb Airfield in Gloucestershire were the icing on the cake.

At the Bog Snorkelling, as I had been awarded £100 as a 'Cool Over 60', a representative of Powergen Staywarm and a photographer accompanied me. I was certainly cool although not in that sense of the word. I had felt not a little foolish trudging up a soggy hillside on a wet day wearing only a swimming costume! Fortunately, the organisers rallied round and found me a wet suit. Getting into it was a challenge in itself. Having watched me struggle into it an onlooker commented "You've got it on inside out and back to front"!

The event, sponsored by Ben and Jerry's Ice Cream, attracts a large crowd. I was fed chocolate fudge ice cream before entering the bog 'to keep up my blood sugar level'! I had been advised that it would be very cold and that I would encounter bog fauna like water scorpions but that these are harmless. I know now why I found it heavy going and nearly faltered on the first 60 yards. I was wearing a snorkel and flippers but I did not keep my head down in the water which made it difficult to use the flippers correctly. Fearing that I would not complete the return stretch, I rolled over on my back and experienced no difficulty completing the course. I believe I may have been cheating but no one cared and the people lining the bank cheered me on. My effort was recognised in some of the Welsh media because I was the oldest competitor and the last!

Wing walking! This involves being strapped in a standing position on a strut on the top of a bi-plane. Clambering into position was quite difficult, with warnings to put one's feet in the right place or "you might go through"! For 10 minutes my pilot swooped and soared, coming in low over the airfield to the cheers of onlookers. I wanted to blow my nose but this was out of the question at 100 miles an hour. My ears weren't quite the same for several days afterwards! I'm glad I did it but I have no burning enthusiasm to repeat the experience!

THE FIRST STEP IS THE HARDEST

I've been asked a lot of questions (and have asked them of myself). Why did I do it? Along the way I've learned what everyone already knows . . it is the first step into the unknown that is the hardest. Once I got started and I had a couple of challenges under my belt my confidence surged and I started to enjoy myself. I did not set out to achieve anything out of the ordinary. I merely wanted a peg on which to hang some fundraising and to use this activity as a means of overcoming my disappointment at the failure of the transplant of my kidney to Sarah. Sarah remains my inspiration and I have exceeeded my target of £28,000. My last fund-raising event took place almost to the day of my first challenge a year before. Simon Davies, Professor of Nephrology and Dialysis Medicine at my local hospital, is also Musical Director of The Border Singers. Together they led a 'sing or listen' performance of Handel's *Messiah*. A local music critic commented: 'This was a Messiah that stirred the emotions and awakened the spirit'. There could not have been a more fitting end to my year.

WHAT MOTIVATES ME?

I enjoyed my fund-raising year enormously. I met new people. I had many new experiences and I feel fitter than ever. I may, of course, be in denial about ageing! I may be defending myself against recognition of the decline in capacity which inevitably accompanies entry into one's eighth dec-

ade. Old age is cruelly undemocratic. If you are unlucky, its worst afflictions may hit you while your peers are still enjoying their golden years. Unluckier still to be prematurely old, sans mobility, sans memory, sans anything. I am fortunate to be physically in good shape. Taking up running when I was approaching 50 was probably one of the best decisions I ever made. Essentially, however, I believe I have merely reverted to the kind of person I always have been.

I left school when I was 16. It was wartime and Sally and I were sent away to a boarding school to keep us safe. Somehow or other we secured permission from our parents to have our bicycles delivered to the school so that we could ride home from Surrey to Devon at the end of our final term. This was no mean adventure in those days. In the 60s, I hitch-hiked from Malta to England and, later with a friend, I hitched from Charing Cross to Jerusalem. I visited the Soviet Union and East Germany when it was still behind 'the iron curtain'. I was in Prague during the Prague 'spring'. I was never slow in coming forward when there was an opportunity to travel. At 71 years of age I find that my zest to explore new places is undiminished but I am aware that time is not on my side. I hope to pack in more travel in the next few years and to balance this effectively with a continuing commitment to my community at home.

It is easier to raise money to support local charities than for causes abroad. I have always wanted to balance supporting local voluntary organisations with support for work amongst the poorest of the poor overseas. I needed to keep my fund-raising personal to appeal to as many people as possible. This is why I chose to support two local renal and transplant patient associations with purchasing a kidney dialysis machine for the Salma Dialysis Centre in Khartoum. A year after Frank died, I visited Khartoum with Khalid Ali to meet his family. While I was there I was introduced to the Salma Dialysis Centre where dialysis machines are in operation from 8.00 am until 1.00 am the following morning. The money I raised will go towards a desperately needed machine for dedicated use by patients with hepatitis infections.

Dr Ali, his family, colleagues and I are now friends united in a common endeavour. When this happens stereotypes which often blunt our understanding of 'the other' fall away and obstacles which so often keep people apart cease to exist.

THE FUTURE

The last year has been a life changing and a life enhancing experience. It is now over three years since Frank died and I found myself thinking the other day, 'at last I'm a grown up'. I long to talk to Frank again and I experience rushes of anguish which are hard to explain. But I am comfortable with myself. I can enjoy my life. The only downside is that running is becoming a lot more demanding and I can foresee the time when I will hang up my trainers! Regular exercise has been a mainstay of my life. I may be past middle age but I still don't want to succumb to middle age spread! Will walking be a fitting substitute? Will I have the courage to be more adventurous on my bike? I don't know. At present I am pre-occupied with a forthcoming visit to Ethiopia, travelling independently to visit an educational project in Tigray which I hope to find ways of supporting. I will also find time to visit the source of the Blue Nile and the Rock Churches of Lalibela! Time may not be on my side but I intend to make good use of what there is.

---

etcetera

Should older women be inventing their own traditions, rites of passage and rituals to celebrate age? If so, what should we celebrate and how?

Continuing or developing an activity while acting as a carer for a husband has been a theme in several of the pieces written for this book. Obviously every one develops and should have their own strategies for dealing with the stress of such a situation. Another thread to this theme is the importance of physical activity in maintaining an emotional and spiritual balance in the face of bereavement (and anyone who has ever cared for someone suffering from dementia knows that the sense of loss usually begins sometime before the actual death).

Angela's way of coping with her husband's death got tied up with the life-giving act of organ donation. That's a very powerful connection. Not many of us could – or, to be honest, would want to – hurl ourselves into the kind of dedicated and demanding activities that Angela did but the principle of the lessons learned by her experience are certainly worth considering.

***Angela's Just 70 Challenge* raised money for the following charities:**

North Staffs Kidney Patients Association: NSKPA offers mutual support to people suffering from kidney disease. They assist patients with equipment which they may need and have difficulty purchasing themselves and sometimes assist with the cost of holiday insurance.

- 1 Kenilworth Grove, Newcastle-under-Lyme, Staffs   ST5 0LE

Staffordshire Transplant Association Family and Friends: STAFF promotes exercise and sport amongst all recipients of a transplants and annually sends individuals and teams to take part in the British Transplant Games.

- 10 Cooper Avenue, Basford, Newcastle-under-Lyme, Staffs   ST5 0QG

The Salma Dialysis Centre, Khartoum, Sudan: The Centre, which is only partly funded by government, offers dialysis and occasionally transplants to public patients living in Khartoum.   While the provision of dialysis machines, which are all donated, is free, patients must pay for what is termed 'disposables' and for their continuing medication. The Centre needs a dialysis machine dedicated for the use of patients suffering from hepatitis infections.

African Children's Educational Trust or **A-CET**: is a small independent charity which spends no money in this country on salaries, fund-raising, or professional fees. it operates in Mekelle in Tigray province in northern Ethiopia where particularly vulnerable youngsters, physically or land-mine disabled, civil war or AIDS orphans, or former street children are supported and mentored through their education. Angela visited many of these children and their families in May this year and saw for herself the work being undertaken. Not a penny is wasted. £10 per month covers the cost of educational fees at recognized schools, colleges or universities with living expenses where necessary and extras such as books, clothes and if needed, medical expenses.

A-CET is now branching out to support two rural communities to build a class-room for children who at present are unable to go to school because there are no facilities. Once a class-room is built, the government will provide a teacher.

- FREEPOST MID 25356, PO Box 8390, Leicester LE5 6ZA. www.a-cet.org

THE PAST IS ANOTHER COUNTRY

Hilary Elfick

*Each has his past shut in him like the leaves of a book known to him by
heart and his friends can only read the title.*   Virginia Woolf, (1882-1941)

It's always about timing. That moment, then,
felt free. Only later, like now, when I remember, down

here that first time in the bush, stilled into waking
by a herald not heard of, impossible to imagine

as I lay surprised by light, the currawong
clearing his throat, beginning to sing

before rolling out of ant-columned sheets, checking shirt and shoe
for poisonous spider, watching through fly screen the slow

shuffle of a home-bound wombat snuffling through lace
of sunlit web, claws groping into maze

of burrows, blindly seeking for his mate's
own homely scent, and I left wondering what right

I had to be here, watching, and what shift
of timing and of place had brought me, what drift

of blind, persistent hunger made me come
to this place at this time, like thistledown

with wombat, antechinus, currawong whose fate
had nothing to do with where I was or how, in this odd light

a half-world over. That topsy-turvy choice had felt quite free
but nothing ever is. And who can tell, and certainly not me,

what made me come here, that time, then, to find
the flip-side of myself, my stranger mind.

WOMEN'S LIVES AND LETTERS

Charmian Cannon

Letters have long been an important source for historical researchers particularly for those trying to reconstruct women's lives. The powerful men about which most history has been written have left official documents as they have lived in the public eye; but the lives of women are recorded only in private writings such as personal letters and diaries.

I have two boxes full of family letters, one written by my grandmother Peg between 1901 and 1943 and another from my mother, her daughter, from 1916, onward. They are tied in neat bundles by date. When I started to read them I found they gave an unfolding story of everyday middle class family life in the first half of the twentieth century. Then I started asking myself questions. Why did they persevere so long in their letter-writing? Why did they keep the letters? What was the function of such letters for family life?

These are letters circulated among family members to keep them in touch with each other's news as well as expressing concern or making practical arrangements. I have also found other examples of such letter collections from different social backgrounds and in different periods. An unusual example is of a family who lived in Cornwall in the 1790s. Though minimally educated they conducted an extensive correspondence to maintain contact with scattered family members using friends or relations to carry the letters when possible; but otherwise, in the days before the penny post, spending a quarter of the weekly income on postage to make sure the letters arrived. The person who provided the impetus to keep the letters going was the oldest sister Elizabeth. Women were of central importance in maintaining the social life of the community.

Jane Austen writes scornfully in Mansfield Park of the addiction to writing letters *'which will include a large proportion of the female world'*. There was a burgeoning of women's letter-writing in the 19th century, with the introduction of the penny post in 1840 making the sending of letters affordable to more people. Writing letters seems to have been a habit among families where the women had the time and literacy to indulge in it. In my family this female letter-writing habit was alive and well in the Edwardian period and continued for half a century. My grandmother died in 1947 aged 88. Her middle daughter Daisy joined the letter-writing circle when she married. Besides being a fascinating source of information about their daily lives and those of their families they also made me think about the use of letters as a way into women's lives, and the place they seem to fill in the transmission of family culture.

In order to interpret letters you need to know who wrote them, for what purpose, to whom. And of course it would be good to have the response as personal letters are a reciprocal process. I don't have many responses but I know a lot about everything else specially as the letters themselves are explicit about their purpose and they took a lot of organising. The letters I have are Peg's part in a kind of round robin called the 'Budget' circulated between a group of five siblings, from a Unitarian middle class family, all married, living in different parts of England. They are a kind of 'family pact' in which each contributor must respect the contributions of the others. There are no letters addressed to individuals, except occasional comments on particular items, which are then open to all the others to read. Peg's letters were usually three or four pages long so by the time the collaborating authors had finished it would have been quite a weighty package for the postman. The term 'budget' is used constantly by Peg and spawns other parts of speech, the verb 'to budge' and 'a budge' as an individual letter.

In September 1899 Peg writes: *'I wish success to the Budget idea because sometimes we have gaps in the news of each other's households.'* But by the following year it was in difficulties because her sister was too busy to organise it.

October 14th 1900.' *'Dear People all . . . Now as to the death of the Budget. Would people like to keep it up in a less ambitious form? Because if it had no pretty cover, and aimed at nothing except circulating news and such scraps as were available, I think I could find time to stitch it together with a brown paper cover. . . and get it out on the first of every month . Will people give me their ideas on the subject? Our young people like sending things and the boys usually read the budgets of their Aunts and Uncles. It is a pity that the link should be dropped, . . . I am only Mama, dressmaker and governess, and I do have time in the evenings . . . But if I do it, the Budget shall be thinner and punctual to the period fixed whatever it is . . . Votes for this plan, or against, please . . . Your loving sister Peg.'*

Two weeks later she was able to report: *'This monthly Budget has made great resolutions to start on its travels on the first of every month . . . like a snowball, collecting material as it goes round. It might be a good idea to post it first to anyone whose budge has not arrived, that the missing budge may be added'.*

So the new Budge was launched, and under Peg's editorship it flourished. The contributions came from the three sisters and two brothers (or their wives), and was circulated between them. Her husband's family did not participate.

Undoubtedly Peg was an efficient organiser. There are instructions as to size and thinness of paper used to make sewing pages together easier, and decrease the cost of postage. Peg uses the same kind of paper for forty years. People are thanked for being punctual without prods. *'No prods will be sent to anyone!'* In July 1901 she writes *"The Punctual Editor' waited for the last post but failed to pick up her sister's letter in time. 'Punctual Editor' grieves for this lapse. And apologises.'* She continues in this vein for over forty years commenting at the age of 83, *'You all wrote your December Budge before 1942 was out. I should have, had I not made one and a half pounds of marmalade yesterday evening.'*

So these letters are not spontaneous expressions of feeling, they are a sometimes onerous but important duty, to be

DEFINING WOMEN

carried out even when the writer is busy with small children or domestic chores. This is particularly true in the years from 1900 to 1914, which are the subject of most of my analysis so far. Retrospectively I view these as the Golden Years. Although there were many social and political conflicts at the national level, at Inglefield, the family home, the family circle is intact and a feeling of security and zest permeates Peg's writing. The war and its aftermath changed all that. Knowing as I do 'what happened next' adds poignancy to my reading.

The letters in this period have elements of a diary, chronicling the events of the previous month and indeed are sometimes based on a daily diary used as a reminder. Visitors, states of health, expeditions, the children's development are reported on; all the everyday details of family life. They also have an educational component and often contain riddles and drawings contributed by the growing children sometimes commented on by their uncles and aunts. There are recipes, and occasional scraps of fabric from dressmaking for a judgement as to suitability.

Peg's letters read as though she is speaking to you on paper. They are humorous and fluent. She speaks about books she has read, Liberal politics, her own local charitable activities; but she tries not to be controversial within the family, as 'the budge is only for the dissemination of news really.'

'Only for the dissemination of news.' Not quite. There are expressions of feeling about the illness of wider family members, the death of friends; and on a lighter note at the end of 1900 , *'Dear people all, A Happy New Year to you! May it be free from servant bothers to Edie, may Vi have no falls; Harry get free of his gout, Robbie find Laird* [his dog,] *and Forster get home*

at a reasonable time for dinner!' But there is no place for emotional outpourings such as might happen between intimate sisters in a one-to-one situation; a group respondent flattens out emotion. Even during the 1914 war when the letters take on a more sombre note, the expression of emotion is restrained. Stoicism is expected during war and that is what is manifest. From what I know of the family culture, stoicism was the norm, and introspection considered indulgence.

The Budge is indeed a family pact, and the pact is arrived at through consultation. *'May I have written opinions from everyone?'* Peg requests, on a particular family matter. She may organise the letter-writing project, but she takes care to canvas the views of the others, not only on the content but as to who should have access to it. In November 1903 she has a request from a close Indian friend asking whether it could be passed to him so that he can keep in touch with the family. She encloses a spare sheet of paper asking that her siblings record their views on this. They all reject it . . . *'the Budget should be for family consumption only. Rob's account of Uncle Joe which is so interesting could never have been written if outsiders had to have the Budge.*' So the group decides the boundaries of the readership and the boundaries of the family; making themselves comfortable with their intimacy and what they feel confident they can write about.

Peg's letters may read as though she is talking to you but of course she is not. Letters are not as spontaneous as spoken dialogue. They lack facial expression, gesture, immediate response. They give the writer time to compose, and thus to present herself to her respondents as she wishes. This in turn presents problems for the interpreter, particularly in this case. The overwhelming impression they give is of a positive, busy, educative culture in which Peg is the centre and determining force; she appears always cheerful and active, close particularly to her daughters, controlling their education and contacts, keeping the servants happy, welcoming guests, working in the garden, the house and the local community. But she obviously wishes to present herself in relation to her siblings in this positive way. Idle moments or idle days (if there are any) are not included, nor moods of discouragement. There is humour about her perceived inadequacies, particularly in public speaking or making social calls, but there is no sense that she minds very much. She is socially confident in the sense that her status is assured and so she can afford not to conform. She also makes it easy for the reader to see how she defines herself by the way she signs off in 1900, '*I am only Mama, governess and dressmaker.*' And in 1943, '*Sister, aunt, mother, Peg.*' Although she was a non-militant supporter of women's suffrage and increasingly involved in political and philanthropic work, her self-identification was entirely in terms of family relationships and maternal responsibilities. She was the authority in the household and the organisation of the letters was one of her essential tasks.

If the letters were my only source for constructing a history of the family I would have more difficulty in accepting Peg's accounts as a representation of her life. But I have other personal sources as well. I knew my grandmother as an old woman, was evacuated to her home for a time during the Second World War and constantly met her on family visits. Her portrait looks out at me with a typically quizzical smile at the top of the stairs. Reading her letters brings her back to life even though a younger self is writing. I also knew my mother's relationship with her which was very close, and my mother's personality which was remarkably like hers. This is both a strength and a weakness. It enables me to put the letters into context but it means my reading of them is highly subjective, infused with positive feelings for both women and for my own involvement in the family culture. Virginia Woolf wrote that women think back through their mothers. I certainly do. If I came to them from outside the family, and from a different class background (a dispassionate historian?) maybe I would find them complacent.

But I also wish to stand outside the class and family context and fit my interpretations into a wider sociological/historical understanding. I am interested in the role of key women in the transmission of family culture through the generations, maintaining continuity in times of disruption; and the function of the letters themselves in this process. But it is also inevitably a celebration of what I see as an exceptionally positive family experience in which my mother and grandmother were largely influential. I am writing a historical account of middle class women's everyday life, and their role in the passing on of family culture. But the personality and life story of my grandmother is at the heart of it.

My grandmother died over fifty years ago. A few years before, in 1943, she wrote about her older sister Vi, who was about to go into a nursing home: '*I've just been putting Vi's budges to go for pulp, and no doubt my bundles will go the same way in a few years! We deceive ourselves in thinking that we shall enjoy reading them in our old age. The days are too short.*' So her letters were not intended for posterity but to indulge in a little nostalgia in her later life? Her daughter Daisy had different ideas. She wrapped them up in dated bundles and stored them in the shoe box and labelled them for me. She did the same with her own letters. She died in 1978 age 89. She knew they would interest me and I feel impelled to do something with them before it is too late. Through how many generations do such family mementos lie uselessly in dusty attics until some impatient descendant throws them out, or says: 'What can I do with this?'

Women's letter-writing had obvious immediate functions in keeping communication going between family and friends before the days of telephone and email; but these letters because they are so organised, continue for such a long time, and are communal, have social functions as well. They are an important means of reinforcing family solidarity, and presenting not just the letter writer's self but a kind of 'family self'. They are instalments in a serial story.

Family solidarity may be expressed through the amount of contact, flow of information, and degree of affection between members. The letters confirm all these, not just through defining 'who counts as family,' and by the detailed news, but by the concern shown for each others' welfare and the mutual decisions about what is acceptable content. There are also accounts of family rituals and routines. Christmas Day is often described in detail, ('*we were 19 for dinner . . . the turkey weighed 20lbs.*') Sometimes there are contributions by the daughters about Christmas, the excitement and mystery of it. The annual routine of measuring the five children to find out how much they have grown during the year is recorded. '*Bernard had grown the most . . . over three inches I think*'; family games are described. All this is uncannily like the routines and rituals I experienced as a child, woven into the culture of the next generation by Daisy my mother.

The need to affirm solidarity and ensure continuity is enhanced during the disruption caused by the 1914 war; there is constant anxiety about the two sons, two sons-law and three nephews in service. Much letter space is devoted to tracing the movements of these young men, when they will come on leave, what danger they are in. On the death of one of her sons in France Peg writes of consoling her daughter-in-law . . . '*No husband or brother left and no child to live for. We were cleaning out the china cupboard!* [when she came] *Such are we – work is our best hope . . . all hands to the job before lunch.*'

But the generations continue. By 1918 there is '*no time for house-cleaning with three babies here. The little new lives are coming to cheer the sad old world.*'

'*Work is our best hope.*' The wartime letters are pervaded by a sense of what patriotism demands; women have a duty not to complain, and not to give up hope. However they feel, this is how they ought to behave. But through all the letters in peace as well as war, there is a celebration of 'the way we do things,' a sense of the 'rightness,' of their family life, which I think is central to their sense of solidarity. *'We go on long walks and cycle rides; we don't take taxis; we don't fuss; we are temperate; we have a private language which excludes the non-initiated. This is how we are, and how we want to be.'* It is repeated in Daisy's letters written between the wars when she has just set up house with a young family. She laughs at her inadequacies as a housewife, is aware of the proximity of neighbours to her small semi-detached home. She writes to her mum, *'Bother the neighbours say I! We're going to live our own life on our own plot of earth in the way we think fit!'*

The writer of the Budge and her letter-writing daughter after her, express a strong sense of self, and a strong sense of family identity and cultural continuity. In May 1943 Peg writes after her brother's death: *'Dear People, You are dwindling in number, but the clan goes on with the young people. Only three of the Sacred Five left to write a Budget.'*

So the letters confirm and make explicit the family culture. They are also part of it. Daisy's letter-writing habit never left her and she was as well organised as her mother. I remember that in the 1950s when we children were grown up she kept a list of family members and friends in her writing case to make sure she didn't forget whose turn it was to get a letter. Absent adult children received a letter once a week. Sunday afternoon was letter-writing time. A friend of mine recalls saying to her: *'I can only write letters when I feel like it.'* My mother looked at her firmly and said: *'It has to be done so you do it.'*

I am sometimes asked whether I carry on the family letter-writing tradition with my own siblings and children: the answer is of course that I don't. Although we are quite a close family and I have written to them all at intervals in the past I never do now. So much has changed. I pick up the phone to find out how they are. My grandmother had no phone until the inter-war period and then remained quite scared of it; much as the older generation today might be scared of some aspects of electronic technology. It took me some time to get used to email, but I have found it invaluable in communicating with my children specially if they are travelling in distant places. I try to write emails as if they are letters. But as for texting . . . !

My mother and grandmother had domestic help and never worked except in their homes. Part of that work was writing letters. I always worked full-time when my children were young and had little help. This increase in women working has been accompanied by more or less universal literacy; but also by changes in family patterns. Families are smaller, more complex, with step and half siblings. They are probably more widely scattered geographically but on the other hand they can be contacted instantly. This must make for a different kind of communication, a conversation rather than the considered presentation I find in my grandmother's letters. I wonder how other women experience family communication in the electronic age? Is it women who write the emails, as they used to write the letters? Is there such a thing as an institutionalised family email?

I try to keep significant family emails to keep the record going. But by the time I've got my collection they will be superseded by text messages on the mobile phone.

etcetera

If you know of any family letter collections like the one described Charmian Cannon would like to hear about them. You can contact her through Third Age Press

Do you agree that women have been the main communicators of family news and transmitters of family culture across generations? Would it be true across class and ethnic cultures? How might this have changed with new family patterns and more women working?

People don't write letters any more. In your experience how has electronic communication affected family communication?

Are emails worth keeping?

Some books about letters

Barton D and Hall N Eds (2000) *Letter writing as a Social Practice: Studies in Written Language and Literacy 9.*

Earle R Ed (1999) *Epistolatory Selves. Letters and Letter Writers 1600 – 1945*

(The above are academic books but with some chapters containing interesting examples)

Kenyon O (1992) *Eight Hundred Years of Women's Letters*

Castor H (2005) *Blood and Roses: the Paston Family in the 15th. century*

Watt D (2004) Ed & trans *The Paston Women: selected letters*

Raverat G (1952) *Period Piece: A Cambridge Childhood*

Young M & Wilmott P *Family and Kinship in East London* – gives a vivid account of the role of mothers in maintaining close family ties in an East London working class community in the 1950s

Cannon C (2003) *Ladies of Leisure ? The Everyday Life of an Edwardian Mother and her Daughters* in *Women's History Magazine* Issue 43 March 2003 – based on the letters written by Peg.

GIFTS OF AGE

astra

write on, write on, they urge with glee,

tell us, tell us, inspire us to see,

to feel and know, sense and share

the gifts of age and how we dare

to do what's not been done before

at least by us: seizing more

than background places,

hushed up faces,

explorations never tasted,

cloistered talents all but wasted,

carnel rumblings still unsated

write on, write on, I hear them shout,

it's not too late to throw off doubt,

dispense with indecision,

unlock the inner prison,

challenge all derision

the way we did in youth

or yearned to do in truth

what is to be engages me

with flights of fancy,

fancied flights beyond

the present sight and sounds

where obligations still abound

and friends are cherished here,

no need for feeling fear,

our zest for life is clear,

we celebrate each year

confidence won't come too late:

the gifts of age

are worth the wait

WOMEN'S TALK

astra

what men call tattle gossip women's talk

is really revolutionary activity

and would be taken seriously by men

(and many women too)

if men were doing the talking

women's talk is women together

probing the privatised

pain isolation exclusion trivialisation

in their/our lives

if situations were reversed

men would react with identical symptoms

to what women feel in their/our gut:

worthlessness self deprecation depression

what men call prattle babble chatter jabber blather

gabbing hot air small talk rubbish gibberish verbosity

clearly tells how language reflects

the deep misogyny that's penetrated our lives

and become common sport

but from this day forward

spare me:

                 I'm sick of being bait

men denigrate our talk at their peril –

that's because they're in ignorance

of its power

our poser,

those precious few of us who see ourselves

as powerful

                serious

                     and deadly

HOMECOMING

Barbara Beer

Where shall it fall – that first touch of the hand,

That caress,

When I am back amid familiar things?

This time it will be night

And only a waning moon to light the path to the house.

In the car

So no chance to fondle chestnut bark

Nor apple tree ridges.

The door keys will not be mine to handle

Nor will the switch which floods the room with light.

Cat is not in his basket:

I cannot stroke his black fur,

Elegant and luxurious

Nor his white chin patch,

Rough and masculine.

Curtains are already drawn

By friendly, house-minding neighbour.

Tray for refreshing tea made ready on the table

With affectionate vase of jasmine –

Yellow-blossomed winter jasmine – by its side.

House-minding neighbour knows as well as I do

Where to find it in our garden.

Accumulated post neatly piled on hall table.

Too late to open now

And before making tea I must go upstairs to the bathroom.

I hang my coat on the hook in the hall

Then turn to climb the stairs and then . . . my hand

Rests on the old, worn, oak newel post at the foot.

This is the moment of recognition

The tactile memory of a lifetime's going upstairs.

First when so small I even could not reach the knob.

Then an adolescent, flying arms barely touching it

As feathered feet went up two steps at a time

From bottom to top.

Or the descent, careful and gracious, of a young bride,

Hand on banister rail all the way down,

Pausing, a white cloud, on bottom step

For Father's sunshine of approval.

A descent more painstaking, with arms' burden of mewling sound.

Again the pause to still the heart

And dry the waiting grandmother's tears.

Many, many journeys up and down.

The newel post which saw them all has a patina

Formed from gentle hands

And sweaty, tennis-playing palms

Or cricket fist flexing an imaginary ball,

Scented fingers lingering while awaiting the doorbell's ring,

Rough gardener's hands leaning heavily after hard toil,

Antiseptic doctor's fingers,

Lithe pianist's drumming rhythms,

Plumbers, engineers, decorators, double-glaziers,

All have used that one strong orb

To help support the loads they carried.

It may be long before I leave this house again.

This homecoming is outstanding

For I have been halfway across the world

To where marsupials hop and birds are red-and-green

And earth is red and inside caves the paintings

Are as old as time –

But now am back amid familiar things.

BEAUTY AND THE BEAST

Maggie Guillon

Women are stupid. There, I've said it. Sorry, but it just burst out. I know it smacks of misogyny and I am, after all, a woman myself. But perhaps that is precisely why I can say it.

Ok, as the phrase goes, let's look at the evidence.

Back in the repressive 1950s I was encouraged to run around topless or even naked, as were many of my friends.

But visit any beach in summer today and you will see tiny tots clad in bikinis. Until adolescence the breasts of girls are no different from those of boys, so why are we sexualising our infants? In fact why do we still submit to hiding our breasts at all? Why, in this post-feminist era, are there increasing numbers of anorexic schoolgirls? Why do we encourage our 'little princesses' to experiment with make-up and affirm these representations through advertising? If we promote the image of our children as miniature adults are we not colluding with the very men who interpret these images as sexual invitations?

Human psychology relies heavily on collective rather than individual thought. As animals we need to reinforce the identity of our pack by demonising and excluding those deemed as a threat to the security of the herd as a whole. Consequently we are subject to witch-hunts and obsessions, and to redefining events and perceptions accordingly. Today's obsession is paedophilia. Yet despite our over-honed analysis of the subject the most obvious connections are rarely made. And heaven forbid that we should attempt to take on collective responsibility.

How many of you reading this will have shaved your legs during the past week? Do any of you still retain the full armpits of the Greenham era? And how many are flinching now at the memory of those hairy harridans who were blamed for the downfall of feminism?

Yet, like the adult male, the adult female has abundant body hair. Its appearance is one of our earliest signs of maturity and is therefore worthy of celebration. Men recognise this and wear their adolescent stubble with pride. If they choose to grow a beard they are not subjected to the abuse reigned upon our local shopkeeper who, as an eighty-year-old crone, sports a complete set of whiskers. Few men spend valuable hours of their lives painfully stripping their legs, and even fewer would display a clean white armpit without some embarrassment. Women on the other hand are urged to fight against adulthood, resist wrinkles with every chemical and surgical means available, hide their unacceptable faces behind a mask of make-up, stay thin rather than ease into the solidity of middle years, and, from the outset, to remove as much body hair as is necessary to deny the maturing process.

Those feminists who exposed this anomaly and had the audacity to alter their body image accordingly, were and still are labelled unsexy – by other women. Today's young women tell me that now they are armed with all the information they can make a free choice, and they freely choose to continue the age-old customs that make them attractive to men. ie. decoration and depilation. Free choice, of course, can never be truly exercised in a culture that bombards us with traditional images of acceptable womanhood. But if we suppose for a moment that it can, why are grown women choosing their own reduction from maturity to a pre-pubescent state? And more importantly, why are we missing the obvious link between this and paedophilia?

Because if men truly prefer their sexual partners to resemble children rather than adult females, what does that say about their subconscious sexual desires? And what does it say about us if we comply?

I am 56. My waistline is expanding, my hair is tinged with grey; thread veins decorate my torso. My face appears mottled and contoured like a three dimensional map of the Alps. If tufts of hair lace the legs of my swimwear and stray wisps peep from under the arms of a T-shirt, young women sneer and giggle. It is hard enough to walk this planet without the added derision of one's own kind.

I look at other ageing women with their lines and creases and see only beauty. I look in the mirror and see only the beast. So what do I do? I shave off my body hair and take up exercise.

I told you, women are stupid.

etcetera

How would you define the term 'post-feminism' and what are the implications for women if the debate is now considered unfashionable?

Is it unreasonable to extend the term 'paedophilia' to describe social convention rather than individual deviant behaviour? If so, bearing the argument of this essay in mind, what term would you suggest as an alternative?

BECAUSE WE'RE WORTH IT . . .
THE SEVEN SIGNS OF AGEING

Dianne Norton

L'Oréal advertises products as attacking the 'seven signs of ageing'. A quick 'google' of the 'seven signs of ageing' elicited 98,000 websites. So what are these blatant portends that identify us as old women?

Apparently most women (surveyed) consistently identified seven relevant signs of ageing.

1. Fine lines and wrinkles
2. Rough skin texture
3. Uneven skin tone
4. Skin dullness
5. Visible pores
6. Blotches and age spots
7. Skin dryness

. . . so anything below the shoulders doesn't matter. Well that's good news isn't it?

. . . and L'Oréal ends every advert with that unctuous ('unctuous', appropriately, is defined in the OED as 'having a greasy or a soapy feel') 'because we're worth it'. What exactly are we worth or perhaps more to the point, what do **they** think we are worth? Presumably the answer to the latter is that we are worth the extortionate amounts it costs to buy their 'anti-ageing' products. They obviously think we owe it to ourselves (and perhaps to anyone who has to look at us) to spend money on products that they claim will halt nature in it's tracks. 'Anti-ageing'? If ever there was an oxymoron – that's it!

So here are my personal thoughts on the seven signs of ageing (in no particular order).

1. THE NUMBERS GAME
Two interlinked things that really make my hackles rise are the media's – mostly newspapers' – obsession with labelling people by age, usually in a completely irrelevant way (will they still be able to do this under the new age discrimination legislation?) and the widespread practise of relating the way a person looks to their chronological age .

'Woman, 63, in fall from Scottish peak' (for the full story see 'Will the Real Joyce Smith stand up . . . page 21) trumpeted the *Wimbledon Guardian*. We read this and instantly dredge up a stereotype of this 63-year-old woman. What on earth, we are meant to reflect, was such an elderly woman doing up a mountain? An interesting fact about this particular story was that only a week later, in the same mountains, a young man was killed in a fall and the press barely noticed. What the press is doing when it uses this device is pandering to our lazy minds or saving themselves the trouble of telling us more about the person and the event in the belief that giving that chronological age automatically gives us a true picture of the person involved.

My second *bête noir* is that statement, or one of its many variations 'but you don't look old enough to be...' and we react with giddy pleasure no matter how hard we try not to because we have been programmed to believe that this is a compliment. However, if we do or don't look a particular age it implies that there is a standard against which we can be measured and if there is a standard what is it and who sets it? Now people who make these remarks are, on the whole, well-intentioned which stops me from making one of several replies that springs to mind. 'Oh', I'd like to say in a deeply apologetic voice, 'I'm so sorry. What am I supposed to look like?' Or it may be more acceptable to say 'but this IS what 66 looks like' or 'but this is what grandmothers look like nowadays'. As I have not had plastic surgery or any other transforming 'procedures' does it not go without saying that what I look like is me at 66 and every other 66-year-old will look like them and, thank heavens, none of us will look the same!

The whole thing about broadcasting our ages – even if the expected coyness of days gone by which made it extremely 'bad form' to mention a 'lady's' age, is changing – or telling us we don't look our age, is that it denigrates us as individuals. It dumps us into the miasma of stereotypical people who are not worthy of individuality and should be faceless and invisible (about which, more anon).

2. SO MUCH FOR 'GREY POWER'

To dye or not to dye – that is the question. I used to be tickled pink by an elderly aunt who would sit with her blue-rinsed hair (sometimes verging on the heliotrope) and get in a lather about young punks and the strange things they did to their hair! However 'the blue rinse brigade' seems to be dying out but there are still plenty of 'cauliflowers' around. But hair colouring is a huge and growing business and not just because people want to cover up the grey but because women of all ages (and an increasing number of men) make a choice to look different. Some women have lovely grey or white or silver hair but for others among us the colour doesn't suit or our grey is dull and lacklustre so we go for something else. It's not that difficult to tell the dyed from the natural so while you might argue that I can hardly claim that hair colour is one of the seven signs of ageing the falsity of it might brand us as one who is not being entirely honest with our looks.

I thought a letter to *The Guardian* a couple of years ago really hit the nail on the head. Hilary Patrick wrote: *I am delighted that the government is beginning to realise that people of 50 are not quite ready to be put out to grass . . . But on behalf of my contemporaries who still consider themselves in their prime, can I gently chide you for portraying me as one of the 'grey vote'. My friends are blonde, some blonder than ever, or bald, but grey, never.*

Does the image that we show to the world affect the way we behave? I used to be a brunette and I think I still think and act like a brunette although, as my hair has faded, I have become increasingly 'blonde'. Yes, I know, I plead guilty to what I complained about earlier – accepting stereotypes – but I think it makes a valid point. I also used to drive a Volvo estate car and when the children started driving themselves we bought a fairly clapped out Ford Fiesta (known to us as a Ford Fiasco). I clearly recall driving it round Marble Arch one busy day and wondering why the experience felt so odd. I realised later that I was driving like

DEFINING WOMEN

a Volvo driver but the other motorists were seeing a Ford Fiesta driver and reacting accordingly. Is this what happens when you change your hair colour?

3. INVISIBILITY

It may seem strange that not being seen could be a sign of ageing but bear with me. Perhaps my feeling about older women's invisibility is related to a lesson I recall from an art class as a child when I was taught how to draw 'negative space' – that is, instead of drawing a person or other figure, you actually draw the space around the figure.

Many older women report that they feel invisible because of their age. We do tend to blame the media – few older women on television, whether as actresses (in anything other than stereotypical parts) or presenters; few good, meaty parts on stage; a lack of strong, older women as role models in business and hence in the press. And the media (to blame them *en masse* as I am about to do may seem hypocritical) does certainly overuse the term 'The Elderly' – as do politicians and others – lumping us all into that grey soup where our individuality doesn't have a hope in hell of flourishing. To make matters worse, they all too often append the word 'burden' to the phrase. The sad dependency of a minority of frail elderly people becomes a seemingly inevitable shadow tainting all our lives and blotting out the positive benefits that the rest of us can bestow on society and the economy.

What we do seem to be getting quite a lot of in the press is publicity given to female celebrities reaching 'significant' birthdays and their success (or lack thereof) in continuing to look young and beautiful. But how relevant is that kind of exposure to us ordinary mortals? And how much of the blame for this invisibility rests on us?

4. UGLINESS IS IN THE EYE OF THE BEHOLDER

I hereby announce the official launch of the 'Campaign for the Freedom of Bingo Wings'. Of course we need a catchy slogan . . . something like 'Flap your bingo wings and fly away'? Seriously though, with the advent of global warming I think the world should get ready for older women becoming increasingly 'cool'. Why should we suffer in the summer just because other people don't like what they see? If the fashion industry continues to produce the most colourful and attractive tops without sleeves, why shouldn't we wear them? There is no reason why older women should be made to feel that their ample underarms are not acceptable other than that other people – other younger people – don't like them. Tough! Perhaps bingo wings are too powerful a reminder of what awaits the young. But think about it. They're not doing any harm. They're not contagious. So why should we feel ashamed or embarrassed? The problem lies with the beholder, not us. And it's so sexist!

As Katherine Whitehorn wrote in *The Guardian* (06.07.06) under the title *Old Age Exposed*: ' . . . *in Italy, a few years ago, some eccentric man suggested that older women should be banned from going topless on the beach, on the grounds that they looked awful – what he got, as I recall, was the appropriate response from women that men with pot bellies should not appear, on the beach or anywhere else, ever, in swimming trunks.*'

So flout your bingo wings – or whatever you fancy – with pride.

5. HANDS, KNEES AND BOOMSADAISY*

While face lifts, breast enhancements, tummy tucks and liposuction seems to be reaching an epidemic scale, there is, perhaps, some satisfaction in the fact that there doesn't seem much that plastic surgeons can do about knees and hands. Much of the argument vented about bingo wings could, I think, equally apply to knees. Now that women are likely to spend more times on their knees doing yoga than scrubbing floors we may be saved from deforming ailments like 'water on the knee' otherwise known as 'housemaid's knee', so why shouldn't we free those knees to enjoy the air.

Now, hands seem to be the final bastion of real age. There's been a lot in the press lately about Madonna's hands – Shock! Horror! They actually look like the hands of a mature woman. Other celebrities have been subjected to analysis (by a Harley Street plastic surgeon, no less) to show that while she was – in the case of Jane Fonda – actually 69 with the face of a 55-year-old, her hands were those of an 80-year-old. If this were true she would be the first truly bionic woman. Scary! Where do they these standards come from? How can anyone who has spent a lifetime examining women's bodies claim that there is some kind of rule clearly setting out what hands or faces will or should look like at any given date?

I was all prepared to wax lyrical on the drooping of the 'boomsadaisy' when I discovered that it probably means hips rather than backside . . . now hips, thereby hangs another tale.

* '*Hands knees and boomsadaisy, I've got a bustle that bends . . .*' originally a Swedish dance involving the bumping of hips.

6. ADVERTISING

Perhaps this is another (like invisibility) negative sign of ageing. We are aware of the absence of real old women in advertisements. A sprightly actress glides up a stairlift or, trim, in her bathing suit, steps easily into a bath especially designed to cater for the less-lissom old woman. Even those magazines dedicated to the 'senior citizen' don't use really old women in their adverts. The relatively young models in adverts wouldn't be caught dead in the clothes they have to wear for the photoshoot. One of my favourites (call me a dirty old woman if you like) shows a young male torso that David Beckham would be proud to call his own, sporting an incontinence 'nappy' (fits waists from 18" to 52")! I wonder what he tells his mates about his 'day job'. The bunionless foot encased in a cosy tweed fleece-lined slipper is attached to a slender ankle and a trim calf unscathed by even the weensiest spider vein. Couples moving into retirement homes may be greying but they are always handsome and brimming with vigour. Catalogues are even worse. Undergarments that look like they belong in a medieval torture chamber are impishly worn by modest sized women perhaps in their 40s. Are we so delusional that we think we will look like these women if we purchase these goods? I doubt it.

A phrase that one occasionally hears and which I think is what these advertisers are trying to get us to buy is 'age appropriate' goods. This is not entirely a bad thing. Obviously there are clothes and footwear that are designed in a certain way as to make them easier to put on or take off, more comfortable or, in other ways, suitable to some people. But this should have nothing to do with so-called 'fashion'. No one should be pressuring us into wearing certain styles of clothing because of our age.

I have also – to my horror – heard 'age appropriate' applied to behaviour? That's just the kind of statement that would cause me to behave in a most outlandish way! Once again, it seems to be a question of someone – but who – trying to set, or assert that there are, standards of dress and behaviour that we all ought to adhere to and that these standards are specific to an age group. Could it be that by herding us into 'appropriate' frocks and shoes and convincing us to behave in an 'appropriate' manner someone is trying to consign us to perpetual invisibility? And why would they do such a thing? Fear, my dears – fear! Maybe that's what it's all about. The young – the male – the powerful (those who, in the majority, control the mega industries of fashion, cosmetics and drugs) are too frightened of their own ageing – the waning of their power – to confront reality.

7. FREEDOM IS ORANGE
(with sincere apologies to those of you who live outside London).

If you live in London, one of the seven signs of ageing has to be that ubiquitous orange plastic cover that comes with your 'Freedom Pass'. I'm certainly not knocking the bus pass – it's a truly wonderful thing. Not only does it save you money but it saves you time and that has to be a good thing as we're running out of it don't forget. Never having to stand in a queue to buy a ticket is true deliverance. However, you are presented with this bright orange plastic wallet which could not proclaim your status any more loudly had been flashing and neon. A side-marker is the little cluster of people standing on the outside of the ticket barriers before the 9 or 9:30 a.m. kick-off for the using of passes (hence the nickname 'twirly' for older people in the capital. 'Sorry, love. You're too early' . . . to get on the bus/train/tube free.)

I've had an idea that I think could be a real money spinner. I'd like to see someone produce a very attractive line in personalised pass covers . . . something tasteful yet sophisticated in velvet with sequins perhaps, or raunchy black leather or fluorescent lycra for the really racy amongst you. The world's your oyster!

The significant thing is that these 'signs of ageing' are promulgated by the non-old. What really matters is what we feel like – what we think is significant – and we mustn't let ourselves be bullied by others – be they advertisers or family – into thinking that something that shouldn't matter to our well-being does. When you hear the ageing actress say 'I may be 97 but I feel 35 inside', remember to shout – even if it's just to yourself – 'oh no you don't. What you feel like is a fit and healthy 97-year-old!' The essential thing is that we learn to be happy in our own skin . . . happy with who we are . . . because we're worth it.

etcetera

What's so special about the number '7'? . . . Seven Deadly Sins, Wonders of the World, Ages of Man according to Shakespeare, Dwarves . . . and now the signs of ageing.

What other signs of ageing bear thinking about?

Why should signs of ageing matter to anyone but ourselves?

Have you ever felt invisible? What can we do to make ourselves more visible?

Why aren't 'real' old people used in advertisements to sell things?

Why should a mature woman suddenly harbour thoughts of buying a new wardrobe with sleeves? It's utterly senseless and all about subtle conditioning. Are women stupid because we accept the fact that fat middle aged men walk around virtually naked with tits twice the size of ours, but we are supposed to conceal everything! Why don't we take back control? Why do we harp back to societies that (allegedly) honoured age yet refuse to do the same in our own?

Why are older male figures such as Dumbledore (the delightful old wizard in Harry Potter) seen as founts of wisdom while women of the same age are merely old witches?

INSIDE OUT

Jan Etherington

In the mirror I can see

A face that looks a lot like me

But older. And somehow less fun.

The outside me is not the one

I feel inside. How can this be?

Inside I'm still young, rude and free.

Inside I haven't changed a bit

From when I studied English Lit

And loved Bob Dylan and the Stones

And wore a bra like ice cream cones.

The inside me is looking out

At some imperious old trout

Who seems to know me. I can't hide

The outside me. But here inside

I'm Lady Chatterley with Mellors

I'm Martha Reeves and the Vandellas.

OLDER WOMEN IN FEATURE FILMS

Rina Rosselson with help from Dr Josie Dolan & Doris Bancroft

> ***Older Women in Feature Films*** was the subject of a Study Day
> organised jointly by the *bfi* and the U3A in May 2006.

This guide has evolved from an interaction between the University of the Third Age (U3A) and the British Film Institute (*bfi*). It has been produced in the spirit of the U3A for the sharing of knowledge.

In 2002 the Brent U3A Film Group decided to devote the year to viewing and discussing films featuring older women. The aim was to learn about film language, whilst exploring our feelings and thoughts about the representation of older women like ourselves. We wanted to compare our experiences of life with on-screen accounts.

Around the time that we were working on these issues, three films with an older woman as central protagonist were released, *Iris* (2001), *Ladies In Lavender* (2004), and *The Mother* (2003). But what of the themes of these films? What images of older women were represented? We have dementia, unfulfilled sexual desires, loss of dignity, and dependence on men whether present or absent. We know that these issues can be very relevant to us as older women, but we also know that they do not represent a complete picture of our lives in the 21st century. So, whilst films like this can be perfectly valid, interesting, entertaining and instructive in themselves, the fact that the only three prominent films about older women to come to our cinema screens in recent years dealt exclusively with negative aspects of ageing, makes you wonder what is going on here.

Our concern and sensitivity to the portrayal of older women in feature films left us asking questions about where and how these films fitted into the general portrayal of older people in the cinema. What about real lives that we would recognise as women who have perhaps lived through WW2, certainly post-war deprivation, the changes brought about by the welfare state, improved educational opportunities for women, the birth of rock and roll, the explosion of ideas and different life-styles in the 60's, feminism, changing relationships between women and men, growing economic independence for some women, equal opportunities for advancement at work, the changes brought about by new technology? We have a lot to say and a lot of stories to tell. We don't deserve to end up in a box marked simply 'old'.

Consequently, in 2005, under the Shared Learning scheme of the U3A, we met with the *bfi*'s Lifelong Learning team in order to explore the possibility of a joint research project about older people in films. It was decided to hold a Study Day at the NFT during Adult Learners Week in May 2006, but beyond that, the nature of the research project was very open.

A research team composed of U3A members of film groups from London Region and the home counties was formed to prepare for the Study Day. At the exploratory phase it became very clear that, the difference between the representation of older men and older women in Hollywood films was so great that we would be unable to adopt this more inclusive, comparative approach. We therefore concentrated on 'older women in film'. In order to place further limits on a fast expanding area of research, we also made the decision to confine our interest to feature films only. It was also necessary to define the term 'older women', since we wanted to avoid the connotations created by films like *The Graduate*. Therefore, we adopted the practice suggested by Age Concern's *Too Old for TV?* (1999), and other research papers which employ the definition of 60+. We felt that the correspondence between this definition and the age range of the research group and the U3A membership was crucial.

In this exploratory stage, we defined the objectives of the project as being:

❀   to review existing research and published literature about films featuring a woman over 60 as the main protagonist, or playing a significant part of an ensemble;

❀   to compile a filmography of popular films, that as comprehensively as possible (within the limits of the project) would identify films in which the main character is an older woman, or in which an older woman is a significant part of an ensemble;

❀   to produce some reviews and case studies of particular films and seek and report feedback from U3A members on these films.

LITERATURE

Research identified several areas of concern, the foremost being the virtual absence of scholarship on older women in film. This is similar to findings made in UN and EU reports on women that recognize the invisibility of the older woman in the media. In terms of film, the invisibility of older women applies to both actresses and characters. As far as older actors are concerned, statistics of actors organisations in the US and UK indicate an ageist bias in the employment of actors, and they also point to a gender gap that gets worse with age.

Women's acting careers seem to suffer from what one writer calls double jeopardy. Not only do actresses receive fewer roles and have less star presence than actors, but this difference increases with age. Contrary to what might be expected following second wave feminism, this pattern has not changed in the USA in the period between 1926 and 1999. Since 1927, 58 men and 32 women over 60 have been nominated for the Academy Awards. Correspondingly, overall roles available to older actors far outnumber those for older actresses . This difference has increased remarkably since the 1960s. A similar pattern exists in the UK. An article in Equity magazine called *'Boys Town: Or How the Feature Film Industry Conspires to Exclude Older Women'* recounts the experiences of British actors. Overall, a general absence of older actresses in film is compounded by a shortage of roles. This under-representation of older women in films bears no comparison to the pattern of the general population.

STEREOTYPES OF OLDER WOMEN

In spite of a huge interest in media portrayals of women by feminist academics since the 1970s, and in spite of demographic changes, the image of the older woman in films has attracted little academic attention. What little research that does exist appears in Sociology and Gerontology publications and only considers American -produced films. Worryingly, even in these academic papers an ageist /sexist bias is sometimes present. Equally, what published work there is into representations of older women in American-produced films, highlights a worrying dependence on stereotypical roles.

The stereotypes reported are:

* The mother: Depending on the historical/social circumstances, she can be wise, strong and loyal, tragic and self-sacrificing. But equally, she can be the overprotective, overbearing, repressive, controlling, suffocating Mom. Recent studies show that in 1990s a new trend seems to be emerging in that the mother is portrayed as suffering some sort of dementia.

* The rich dowager: often a widow, she can be feather-brained, a figure of fun or powerful figure of inflexible authority.

* '... feisty grandmothers, ageing careerists and sharp tongued spinsters of the 1930s.

* Servants, maids, waitresses often of ethnic minority background.

OLDER WOMAN AS PROTAGONIST

In all films, the function of a central protagonist that is psychologically developed and provides the narrative motivation is crucial. On rare occasions the protagonist is an older woman, although this does not necessarily escape stereotype.

The protagonist is frequently a mother stereotype. Ma Joad in *The Grapes of Wrath* is a good example of the strong mother, whilst *Make Way for Tomorrow* and *Lady for a Day* portray the tragic and self-sacrificing mothers.

The menacing 'mom' is present in *The Anniversary*, whilst in *Psycho,* 'Mom' pervades the film with her controlling tyrannical, terrifying presence, even though she is never visibly represented. This last film is interesting in that Hitchcock's downbeat ending reveals the horrific mother to be a construction of the diseased mind of the young man.

From the 50s another type of protagonist appears: the ageing, embittered, sad and grotesque actress. The classic *Sunset Boulevard* (1950) is described sometimes as a metaphor for the end of the studio area in hollywood but there is also *Whatever Happened to Baby Jane?* (1962) and *Fedora* (1978). In *Whatever Happened to Baby Jane?*, we have the psychotic ex-child actress, the embittered spinster career woman and 'mom' all in one film.

Two films, *Arsenic and Old Lace* and the cult *Harold and Maude* have been identified by some U3A members as standing out: in that they unsettle pervasive stereotypes of defenceless, sexless older women. In the former film, two 'little harmless old ladies' turn out to be serial killers. In the second, 'little old' Maude is full of anarchic energy. She inspires in Harold the will to live life to the full, and at 80 initiates him to sex. Even though she ends her life, it does not diminish the impact of her enduring vitality.

The 1980s are often considered as producing a new era for older women in films because three oscars for best actress in a leading role were awarded to Katherine Hepburn (age 74) (*On Golden Pond* 1981), Geraldine Page (age 61) (*The Trip to Bountiful* 1985) and Jessica Tandy (age 80) (*Driving Miss Daisy* 1989). But even though these films employ an older actress, do they really show any change in the representation of older women? In as much as their main theme is ageing rather than the decaying old age of the 60s they are different. But each one still retains some attributes of previous portrayals. Ethel Thayer in *On Golden Pond* is primarily the supporting wife/mother of the 1930s. Also, in *The Trip to Bountiful* the mother/mother-in-law conflict is once again placed under scrutiny. But the new theme of nostalgic need to visit one's past is explored and the obstinate older woman is not rich. However there is a suggestion of early dementia in the acting that deprives the woman of any sort of dignity, and reduces her strength of character to a disease of aging, rather than a trait of feminine strength. Finally the rich dowager is here in *Driving Miss Daisy* although not as inflexible as before as she changes her racist attitudes. In one way it is a new departure in that the female lead is Jewish and the male lead black. They are seen in a social/historical context and are not one-dimensional. But the film could well symbolise the double standard in the representation of ageing. The chauffeur who becomes the carer remains competent as he ages while the woman loses her autonomy and control. The film also makes it safe to represent a mixed relationship since the older women is de-sexualised.

Twenty years on from the shifts of the 1980s three British films, *Iris* (2001), *Ladies in Lavender* (2004), and *The Mother* (2003) that provided the motivation for this project were released. The representation of older women in British films has received even less attention than their American counterpart. Indeed, if we take Hollywood as a national cinema, it is the only one to have inspired the kind of research of interest to this project. Existing research on 1930s British films does identify older women as being typed as difficult dowagers who are typically eccentric. They are largely confined to comedies and *Old Mother Riley*, a drag performance, is also quoted in this category. Also, in British films, the little old lady in *The Ladykillers*, the eccentric nanny/spy of *The Lady Vanishes* and the many impersonations of Miss Marple present us with autonomous older women outside any family relationships. But how far these representations are typical of British films has yet to be explored in the academic context.

Whilst brilliant older women get star billing in films like *Iris, Ladies in Lavender, and The Mother*, the roles they perform do no justice to the lives and aspirations of older women, nor do they represent the contributions they make to society. In these films there is no sign of our changing world, nor of the diversity of the population of modern Britain. Whilst the proliferation of incidental characters with dementia, and *Iris*, a major film showing the descent into Alzheimer's disease of a brilliant female intellectual, could be interpreted as a representation of social reality, they can also be seen as expressing a new fear of ageing in the mainly young, male media executives. Consequently, they do little to address the absence of older women's lives on our screens. Similarly, the nostalgic return to a genteel (class bound) idyllic time in 'postcard' Cornwall of *Ladies in Lavender* provides comfortable viewing. The two sisters who live by the sea and the gentle pace are reminiscent of the American film, *The Whales of August*. But

DEFINING WOMEN

in *Ladies in Lavender* one of the women is unbalanced by her unfulfilled motherly/sexual needs. In *The Whales of August* the women are autonomous. *The Mother* has been hailed as a breakthrough because it depicts an older woman having explicit sex with a much younger man. This time we have a selfish 'mother as victim' liberated by having sex with her daughter's lover. A majority of respondents in our research project found the character unsympathetic and it was the least liked of the eight films of our survey.

In 2005, two films, *Mrs Henderson Presents* and *Keeping Mum*, were released. The former again features an eccentric rich dowager. In the latter, a black comedy, a murderous Maggie Smith subverts the mother, grandmother, housekeeper stereotypes.

While waiting for the establishment of the film industry to discover the richness and diversity of older women's lives we can remain alert to the issues around stereotyping and ageist practices within the film-making industry highlighted by existing research into representations of older women and film. The research for a filmography is still a work in progress but it has been instructive. There are some films which are relevant to our times that are intellectually challenging or just entertaining. The films we looked at may not be readily available but they can be obtained second hand, or recorded from TV – more often than not broadcast very late at night.

The tragic inability of coping with growing older is the subject of the French classic *Le Chat*. There are life review and reminiscence films like *Fried Green Tomatoes*. Minor comedies *Alive and Kicking* and *Mrs Caldicott's Cabbage War* show the empowerment of residents of retirement homes. For shocking effect of a sexual nature, Jeanne Moreau in *The Old Lady Who Walked in the Sea* cannot be surpassed. Two Australian road movies and one Brazilian (*Over the Hill, Spider and Rose, Central Station*) deal with self-discovery, growing friendship with a younger man and faith and change respectively. The Canadian film for which much of the dialogue was scripted by the actresses, *The Company of Strangers* – the title of this film was later changed to *Strangers in Good Company*– (a scene from which is depicted on the previous page) exposes the diversity of women's background and experience, their friendship and resourcefulness. *Innocence* and *Les Temps Qui Changent* portray the breakdown of a marriage. *Unhook the Stars* sees the mother liberating herself from her children. The effect of a mentally disabled woman on her three sisters is told gently in *Pauline and Paulette*. The strong, competent and caring matriarch is still present in *Antonia's Line*. The controversial *Tatie Danielle*, raises many questions around ageism. In *A Woman's Tale*, Sheila Florance, who was dying of cancer herself, portrays a woman full of dignity, wit and humour in the face of death. The compassionate, respectful caring of her nurse is also very important and could well be used as a model for trainee nurses. *Fear Eats the Soul* is considered a classic. The protagonists, a 60-year-old cleaner and a younger Moroccan immigrant worker are lovers and get married. They are set against an atmosphere of ageist and racist intolerance. And last but not least is the great *Tokyo Story* which so delicately portrays the acceptance of the imperfections of family relationships, and the experience of time passing and loss.

WHAT HAPPENED NEXT

The group responsible for organising the U3A/*bfi* Study Day was an *ad hoc* working team . However a new project is being planned.

The 2006 Study Day also saw the publication of an online guide:

(www.bfi.org.uk/filmtvinfo/library/publications/litresearch.html).
This guide is a free download.

Two groups now form the Brent U3A film group. One is open to all local members and is based at the Tricycle where they meet to view and discuss the films screened on Thursdays matinees. A smaller group, composed of six women interested in the representation of older women in films, is the origin of the U3A/ *bfi* project. This group is a closed group at the moment as the members have already started working on a new project.

CONTACTS: Brent U3A

To join Brent U3A and the Tricycle group: 020 8961 3004
For U3A film groups: Rina Rosselson: rinaross@mac.com or 020 8902 0655
Dorrie Bancroft: doris.bancroft@btopenworld.com or tel 020 7624 6791
See Page 148 for information on U3A in the UK and how to locate local groups.

BRITISH FILM INSTITUTE (*bfi*)

The new *bfi* Southbank on the site of the National Film Theatre opens in 2007. Screenings and events aimed at older audiences will form part of the ongoing programme. Details of these will be available through the *bfi* website or from the *bfi* Education team.

CONTACT:
Marysia Lachowicz, *bfi* Education
21 Stephen Street, London W1T 1LN
020 7957 4787
www.bfi.org.uk
education@bfi.org.uk

etcetera

Did you know that 97% of films screened in the UK are made in the USA or are joint USA/UK productions? What hope then of interesting distributors (for they are the ones that hold the power) to take an interest in films about older women?

Can you conceive a plot for a film that would represent 'a complete picture of our (older women) lives in the 21st century'? Can you think of a book about older women that would make a good film?

Are 'ordinary' lives interesting enough to be made into mainstream films?

One of the contributors to the Study Day represented a small community cinema in Somerset which regularly showed films followed by discussions. Is there any way we could persuade local cinemas (even the multiscreen giants) to put on similar events?

WHERE WE ARE NOW

Maggie Guillon

'. . . if a woman is healthy she lives to grow old; as she thrives, she reacts and speaks and shows emotion, and grows into her face. Lines trace her thought and radiate from the corners of her eyes after decades of laughter, closing together like fans as she smiles . . . in a precise calligraphy, thought has etched marks of concentration between her brows, and drawn across her forehead the horizontal creases of surprise, delight, compassion and good talk. A lifetime of kissing, of speaking and weeping, shows expressively around a mouth scored like a leaf in motion. The skin loosens on her face and throat, giving her face a setting of sensual dignity. Her features grow stronger as she does. She has looked around in her life, and it shows . . . She is darker, stronger, looser, tougher, sexier. The maturing of a woman who has continued to grow old is a beautiful thing to behold'.

Naomi Wolf   *The Beauty Myth*

I begin with the above passage because Naomi Wolf's vision of age is a delightful and necessary antidote to our modern era of 'newth'. To be old in this new, young century, is to be viewed as obselete, as unlovable. Despite decades of feminist theory and practice, despite classics such as 'Fat is a Feminist Issue' and 'The Beauty Myth', women are as vulnerable to negative imagery as ever. Still unable to celebrate the gift of ageing, we shave and paint our bodies, mutilate them and fill them with chemicals, all in a desperate bid to resemble the unformed vacuity of youth, to erase the poetry of a maturing life.

In such a hostile atmosphere menopause can be a confusing experience. On the one hand strong women are indeed celebrating their release from the monthly cycle and embracing a freedom of spirit which is both enabling and empowering. On the other hand society is advocating plastic surgery and HRT, and neutralizing our already bridled voices by rendering us invisible or irrelevant after a certain age. We all know that if men truly experienced the pausing of the menses the whole structure of society would alter accordingly: support systems would be set up in the work place to counterbalance memory loss; tools would be redesigned to be undroppable; special air-conditioned rooms would be set aside for hot flush relaxation periods. But in this post (read 'illusory') feminist era the best we can hope for is a shared empathy fuelled through openness and humour.

The thing about growing older is that all those little alterations you swore would never happen begin to take place. You knew beyond a shadow of doubt that you would never, ever wear reading glasses on a chain around your neck. Then one day you look up and (squinting with difficulty into the mirror) notice that for some reason you resemble Edna Everage. OK, it might be a tangled bit of coloured rope instead of a gold chain, but the effect is the same. How did it get there?

In case you haven't joined us yet, these are the early signs. Over the years you hold objects further and further away from the end of your nose until your arm just isn't long enough. The next stage is when you find yourself accosting young(er) people in shops and asking them to read the small print on labels for you. Those half moon fashion statements which made bold men quiver as you peered over them in staff meetings and which were left casually beside Booker prize winning novels, sud-

denly become as essential as breathing – if they leave your side for an instant you cease to function. And it's then, naturally, that they decide to go missing at every opportunity. Hours that could have been better spent writing your own novel are consumed in frenzied searches of the planet. So what price a bit of string? As with most things menopausal, it's a choice between two or more embarrassments.

A pair for reading, a pair for distance or, if you are lucky, just for driving, sun glasses, reading sun glasses... (the latter presupposes some readers do not live in Britain). Large rucksacks become indispensable. Note: this sudden influx of extra items coincides with a decreasing ability to either see or remember them.

The kitchen is a danger area for a menopausal women. It is also pretty hazardous for those around her. Ann was cooking a delicious sauce which needed pepper. She picked up the pepper mill, looked at it, couldn't think why it was in her hand, so re-filled it with peppercorns and put it back on the shelf. She made the sauce, covered it with tin foil and cooked it. Then she remembered.

At least she remembered.

Jane was about to cook a meal for friends and was waiting for the oven to heat up. She noticed that the light was out, assumed it had reached the right temperature, placed the food inside and joined her friends in the other room. When she came to serve the meal she discovered that she had never put the switch on in the first place and had an ice cold oven full of ice cold, raw food.

Having learned from this experience, the next time her friends called she was careful to check the switch twice. The light went out and she placed the food inside. When she went to examine its progress she found

DEFINING WOMEN

an empty oven. She had put the food back in the fridge.

Menopausal wipe-outs can be entertaining, (no, they can, really), assuming of course that they don't take place at the front of a lecture hall or start to resemble minature black-outs at the wheel of a car. They can provide older women with a common thread of laughter and, through shared experiences, dispel any remaining fears of being alone, demented, or stupid. No-one is negating the dangers involved in leaving a 6 month old grandchild on the bus. But if we are proud to be crones we cease to be distracted by shame or anxiety, and instead of 'them' laughing at us, we are laughing loudest, with each other. Let's transform our crankiness into *joie de vivre* – what better way to feel young!

etcetera

How can women effectively celebrate age in an ageist society?

Why, in your opinion, do women still choose to accept negative images of themselves by capitulating to their demands? Is it the persuasive subtext of reward or the anxiety of rejection? Or both?

Is there any merit to the hypothesis that women are innately masochistic?

How important is it to have a sense of humour about growing old?

ORGANISATIONS OF INTEREST TO OLDER WOMEN

Some of the organisations listed here are specific to older women, others to women of all ages while some will be of interest to older men as well as women.

If you know of other organisations that would be of interest to older women please send details to Third Age Press, 6 Parkside Gardens, London SW19 5EY or dnort@globalnet.co.uk

For up-to-date contact information for these organisations check the website

www.wwwow.info

GROWING OLD DISGRACEFULLY

Growing Old Disgracefully is a Network of support and friendship for older women, based in the UK but with membership open worldwide. It is not about being 'disgraceful' in the old conventional sense. We use growing old disgracefully as a challenge to the image of 'growing old gracefully' which implies that as old women we must be silent, invisible, compliant and selflessly available for the needs of others.

The network is about growing: growing old alongside other like-minded women, growing old into our best selves, breaking down personal barriers, finding companionship and fun; but most of all helping to change our own and society's attitudes to women's ageing.

The annual subscription is now £15 ... but you get a lot for your money:

- ❀ A quarterly Newsletter
- ❀ A complete list of members' addresses
- ❀ Access to national meetings & residential workshops
- ❀ An opportunity to join one of the countrywide local g.o.d. groups
- ❀ A bursary fund available for members who might otherwise be unable to take part in Network activities

CONTACT: Daphne Ritchings
33 St John's Road
Pleck, Walsall
WS2 9TJ
01922 625589
www.growingolddisgracefully.org.uk
info@growingolddisgracefully.org.uk

OLDER FEMINISTS NETWORK

The OFN was formed in 1982 and has met regularly ever since in order to give voice to the the concerns of older women which we felt were being ignored in feminist circles and in society generally.

The OFN aims:

- To counter the negative stereotypes of older women in society
- To challenge the combined ageism/sexism which older women suffer
- To provide contacts, mutual support and exchange of ideas and information
- To mobilise the skills and experience of older women in campaigning for a better deal

Activities: We meet monthly in Central London with speakers, workshops and shared lunch and we have a winter party. Our bi-monthly Newsletter goes out to older women throughout the UK, Europe, North America and even Japan.

All older women are welcome at our meetings, 'older' being self-defined.

CONTACT: astra
54 Gordon Road
London N3 1EP
020 8346 1900
bmdouglas@supanet.com

THE RED HAT SOCIETY

The Red Hat Society was started in America by Sue Ellen Cooper and inspired by the well-known poem *'Warning'* by Jenny Joseph. The idea of finding time for fun and frivolity after fifty has great appeal for those of us who have spent so much time looking after the needs of others. There are now over 40,000 chapters world wide. Most have been started as a result of seeing a group of red hatters out and about. It has also provided a wonderful opportunity to meet ladies from all over the world who have a common bond.

The Red Hat Society began as a result of a few women deciding to greet middle age with verve, humour and elan. We believe silliness is the comedy relief of life, and since we are all in it together, we might as well join red-gloved hands and go for the gusto together. Underneath the frivolity, we share a bond of affection, forged by common life experiences and a genuine enthusiasm for wherever life takes us next.

Who are we? What do we do?

We are the women in the red & pink hats. We are the mothers, grandmothers, and daughters of society. Little girls grow up, but they're never too old to play dress-up and have tea parties.

The standard answer to the question, *'What do you do?'* is . . . Nothing. Our main responsibility is to have fun! We see this group as an opportunity for those who have shouldered various responsibilities at home and in the community their whole lives, to say goodbye to burdensome responsibilities and obligations for a little while. The refrain of the popular Red Hat Society theme song puts it rather bluntly: *'All my life, I've done for you. Now it's my turn to do for me.'*

Are there any rules?

The Red Hat Society calls itself a 'dis-organization', and we are proud of our lack of rules and by-laws. We have also discovered a 'mission' of sorts: to gain higher visibility for women in our age group and to reshape the way we are viewed by today's culture. We are decidedly UN-strident, but we hope to advance our agenda with good humour and laughter. We are working to build a dis-organization within which we can all connect and eventually take over the world!

The spirit of the Red Hat Society forbids rules, per se. There is, however, ONE inflexible guideline that we must insist upon: You must be a woman of 50 or over (or you may be a Pink Hatter under 50), and you must attend functions in full regalia, (red hat, purple outfit for women 50 and over, or pink hat and lavender outfit for women under 50).

There is no central organisation in the UK. The website below lists the location of chapters but gives no contact details.

CONTACT: http://www.britishredhatters.ik.com. Several local UK chapters do have their own websites. www.redhatsociety.com takes you to the home site (which is American) but you can find some local details if you search there for chapters in England.

AGLOW

Association of Greater London Older Women [AGLOW] is a voluntary membership organisation for women over 50. The objectives are to bring together older women to discuss issues affecting them, to raise a collective voice and counter age discrimination, racism, sexism and homophobia.

They organise four or five conferences per year on topical issues by sharing information and experiences.

They support and celebrate relevant events such as Black History Month and International Women's Day.

Through their Performances Programme members write and perform sketches based on their own experiences to raise awareness of pertinent issues such as ageism and sexuality. These are performed to interested groups and at relevant events.

With sessions on assertiveness and communication, AGLOW aims to enhance older women's confidence and give them the opportunity to make their voices heard.

CONTACT: Association of Greater London Older Women [AGLOW]
6 – 9 Manor Gardens
London N7 6LA
020 7281 3485
info@aglowlondon.org.uk

OLDER WOMEN'S COHOUSING

Does the following conversation seem a familiar one? 'What shall we all do when we are old? Shall we get together and share our living arrangements? Why don't we run our own 'old people's home'?' This is a common topic for very many women in their fifties who, anticipating more than a third of their life to come, are wondering how best to shape it so as to stay happy, active and companionable.

Members of the Older Women's Cohousing [OWCH] in London have moved past the idle fantasies that usually accompany this discussion to do something about a practical solution. We have adopted a model developed by older people in Denmark and The Netherlands and are planning a cohousing community where each will have her own front door but will live as part of a self-managing, mutually supportive group. It will be the first of its kind in the UK specifically for our age-group and for women.

The essence of cohousing is that members build a sense of community through a shared project, thus getting to know each other and coming to an agreement about common values and goals. The community we are building will be based on acceptance and respect and sharing of responsibility plus a balance between privacy and community. We want to counter ageist stereotypes by remaining firmly in charge of our own lives, co-operating with each other in a way that recognises individual strengths. We have policies about such issues as equal opportunities, conflict resolution, mutual support, pets etc. and we publish a quarterly newsletter. We welcome new members of all ages above fifty, as we know we will need more women than places in order to be sure of filling them when the time comes.

Current plans are to develop a block of 24 flats with shared facilities like a common room, guest room, laundry etc and a garden in an area of London near to shops and other amenities and public transport. Those who can will purchase a flat, others will part buy/part rent and those who are eligible for social housing will apply for the tenancies of rented flats which are subsidised by a housing grant. Phase two will be developed along similar lines elsewhere in London. Besides our own subscriptions, we are funded by a Trust for running costs over the next two years and we hold a pan-London Social Housing grant for our building. We are a company limited by guarantee.

CONTACT: Older Women's Cohousing [OWCH]
PO Box 44628
London N16 8WH (send A4 sae)
www.owch.org.uk
info@owch.org.uk

GRANDPARENTS PLUS

Grandparents plus – sharing good practice for children and the extended family

Grandparents plus raises awareness of the valuable role of the extended family, promotes kinship care and supports people working with vulnerable children and their families.

Grandparents plus has a bimonthly newsletter which is sent to friends and supporters.

Anyone interested in learning more about this work should contact the office to ask for regular copies of our newsletter. Leaflets and reports about issues facing grandparents are also available, such as *Learning with Grandparents*, as is a special newsletter for grandparents who are raising their grandchildren called *Grandparents First*.

CONTACT:
Grandparents plus
18 Victoria Park Square, London E2 9PF info@grandparentsplus.org.uk
020 8981 8001 www.grandparentsplus.org.uk

GRANDPARENTS' ASSOCIATION

The Grandparents' Association services include an advice and information line, welfare benefits advice, publications, support groups, and Grandparent and Toddler groups and mediation. They are actively recruiting new members and training volunteers to expand these services.

Contact the Advice Line to speak to friendly advisers – they offer a listening ear and a confidential and efficient service. They can refer you to our Advice Line Co-ordinator for help on issues that concern grandparents today or their mediation service.

CONTACT: Grandparents' Association
Moot House,
The Stow,
Harlow,
CM20 3AG
01279 428040
Helpline: 0845 4349585 info@grandparents-association.org.uk
www.grandparents-association.org.uk

CRUSE BEREAVEMENT CARE

Anyone can contact Cruse if they want to talk about themselves or someone they know who has been affected by a death. Cruse Bereavement Care exists to promote the well-being of bereaved people and to enable anyone bereaved by death to understand their grief and cope with their loss. The organisation provides counselling and support. It offers information, advice, education and training services including specific information on:

- What to do when someone dies
- What can help
- Coping with a crisis
- Useful publications

CONTACT:
Cruse Bereavement Care
Cruse House, 126 Sheen Road
Richmond, Surrey
TW9 1UR
Administration: 020 8939 9530
Fax: 020 8940 7638
General Email: info@cruse.org.uk

Day by Day helpline 0870 167 1677
or Email us at: helpline@cruse.org.uk

HAGSHARLOTSHEROINES

www.hagsharlotsheroines.com is a worldwide community of writers where you can publish your work and develop your creative writing skills. We accept fiction and non-fiction and can provide feedback and writing tips that are particu-

larly focused on writing about women. Membership is free and provides full access to the website and the opportunity to sign up for our monthly newsletter.

Our Writer's toolkit is a wonderful resource of writerly wisdom from how to use the internet for research to the perils of self-publishing. The toolkit additionally features motivational interviews with women writers who share their creative secrets with hagsharlotsheroines.com.

We also aim to entertain and inspire with our extensive range of hagsharlotsheroines tales. From Lucretia Borgia to Boudica we publish work that unshackles women from stereotype. Inspiration combined with information is also to be found in our Book Club area where we offer detailed book reviews across the genres.

Keeping members up-to-date is important to us and we aim to keep you on the trail of the latest competitions, events, and writing workshops. Moreover, being a website we make sure we find you plenty of interesting writing-related websites to click through.

hagsharlotsheroines has grown since its original concept of writing about women from history, legend and myth. Though we will always be fascinated by herstory we know how important it is not to let history define us, or importantly, to limit our creativity.

We are now exploring new literary landscapes and actively welcome quality creative writing on all themes, in all genres to explore issues of gender and identity. We still want stories about our pasts but also our futures too.

We hope you will join us at www.hagsharlotsheroines.com.

CONTACT:
Laura Wilkinson laura@hagsharlotsheroines.com
Helen Wilkinson helen@hagsharlotsheroines.com
Kim Rooney kim@hagsharlotsheroines.com
Tel: 0870 770 3294

Genderquake Limited, (a sister site to hagsharlotsheroines) is an ideas-based enterprise which provides creative solutions, strategic counsel, and capacity building services to enable individuals and organisations realise their potential. They have particular expertise in the

gender dynamics of social, economic and technological change and their core client base includes women entrepreneurs, the self-employed, small business, and the not for profit sector including charities, social enterprises, and think tanks.

www.genderquake.com

My Heroines is a new voluntary association and runs creative writing and self development workshops for children, young people and life long learners. Their aim is to promote, develop and advance human potential through education and creativity exercises through the arts, including creative writing and facilitated personal development workshops, on My Heroines themes in out of school clubs, youth centres, and adult learning centres throughout the UK. My Heroines is the charitable arm of www.hagsharlotsheroines.com and Genderquake Limited.

laura@genderquake.com. for more information.

RUSKIN COLLEGE

Ruskin College provides educational opportunities for adults with few or no qualifications. They aim to change the lives of those who need a second chance in education. Ruskin welcomes students who not only want to develop themselves but also want to put something back into society. Ruskin offers a special range of Women's Studies and activities for all ages.

CONTACT: Ruskin College,
Walton Street
Oxford OX1 2HE
01865 554331
General queries: enquiries@ruskin.ac.uk

Women's Studies: Katherine Hughes
01865 554331
khughes@ruskin.ac.uk

RANSACKERS

Ruskin College also hosts the Ransackers project.

The Ransackers project provides an opportunity for people over the age of 55, who have a positive view about 'growing' older and have not previously benefited from further education. Participating Students spend one term at one of the colleges participating in the project and with the help of a tutor, produce an independent original research project in an area of personal interest.

Participating Colleges
Coleg Harlech (Wales)
Plater College (Oxford)
Ruskin College (Oxford)
Newbattle Abbey College (near Edinburgh)
Hillcroft (women only) (Surrey)

CONTACT: Liz Mathews
01865 517820
lmathews@ruskin.ac.uk

THE FAWCETT SOCIETY

Fawcett is the UK's leading campaign for equality between women and men. We trace our roots back to 1866, when Millicent Garrett Fawcett began her lifetime's work leading the peaceful campaign for women's votes. Our vision is of a society in which women and men enjoy equality at work, at home and in public life. We campaign on women's representation in politics and public life; pay, pensions and poverty; valuing caring work; and the treatment of women in the justice system. We make real differences in women's lives by creating awareness, leading debate and driving change. Our lobbying power means we have real influence right at the top of UK politics and among those who make decisions. Our successes range from a change in the law to allow political parties to use all-women shortlists to increase the number of women MPs, to reform of the rape law, to a new duty on public bodies to promote equality between women and men.

In the 1980s The Fawcett Society launched a rallying call, a Women's Action Day. This was spearheaded by Mary Stott, former Fawcett chair and editor of the Guardian's Women's Pages. This event brought together representatives of nearly 70 organisations with a membership of at least a million members, and signalled Fawcett's transformation from an extremely well-respected, but comparatively little-known body, to the professional and better-known organisation that we are today. The Women's Service Library went on to become a large and impressive collection, which has since been re-housed in the purpose-built Women's Library.

As a campaigning charity, we are always in need of financial support and you can give this by joining or donating to Fawcett.

CONTACT: Fawcett Society
1-3 Berry Street
London EC1V 0AA
020 7253 2598
www.fawcettsociety.org.uk

RAGING GRANNIES (CANADA)

The Raging Grannies began in Victoria, British Columbia, in 1987 when a group of women, active in the peace movement, sat down in Bess's living room and decided they needed a new way to wake up the world. They'd adopt a new persona – crazy old ladies in crazy hats – and instead of preaching – they'd sing, but sing satiric songs. Their targets would be anyone threatening peace and they'd go anywhere – best of all where they were not invited. They didn't want to be 'entertainers'.

From peace issues, their focus grew to include the environment and social or economic justice and they would try to adopt the First Nations'* principle of thinking in terms of seven generations to come. Quickly, the movement spread by word of mouth and press coverage so that there are now more than 70 'gaggles', most of them in Canada or the USA but we are also scattered as far away as Greece, Israel and Australia.

The Victoria gaggle includes Inger, who fought in the Danish resistance against Hitler (but was a hopeless shot with a gun!); Betty, who was an electrician's helper in the Vancouver dockyard, building warships; Fran and Laura, who came to Canada from the USA because of the Vietnam War; Ruth, who taught at Yale and was also a member of the Black Panthers (she's white!); Alison, who got expelled from university at 17 for protesting and spent a lot of time in Central America, helping guerrilla groups. One of our high moments here was protesting the clear-cut logging of Clayoquot on the west coast of Vancouver Island. Inger and Alison went to jail and the rest of us were valuble supporters of the blockade.

Other moments? Holding a tea-party aboard a US nuclear battleship, having a lovely row with the captain and being escorted off ship with much publicity. Closing down our provincial legislature by standing up in the House to call out, successively 'Affordable Health Care for Everyone'. That was three years ago and we are still banned from the House.

We've travelled all over Canada, singing and protesting and are recently back from a visit to Cuba, sponsored by the Movement for Peace. We hold weekly meetings and practices. Each meeting includes a very short chance for each member to report how she's doing personally, but no whines. If you're out of hospital, that's fine, let's get on with it.

We don't sing well; in fact we are famous for it! Everyone who wants to sing, sings, however badly she does it. We recently contributed to a CD being put out by the Granny Gaggles.

A few of the Victoria Grannies remember their Grannies as role models (as fighters for women's rights, for example), but most of us don't look back at all. We don't keep memory books. We've lost our old photos. We look forward to making the world a better place and we'll do so till we kick the bucket. And then we hope our ashes will make fine fertilizer.

* Canada's native people

CONTACT: Alison Acker
#5, 851 Wollaston Street
Victoria, BC
Canada V9A 5A9
alisona@pacificcoast.net

GRANDMOTHERS FOR PEACE INTERNATIONAL

OFF THEIR ROCKERS?

Grandmothers for Peace, a non-profit organization, was formed in the USA in 1982 at the height of the Cold War. Since then our work has expanded to include the dangers of nuclear power plants; radioactive waste; sub-critical and computerised nuclear testing (now that underground testing has been banned); the nuclearisation and weaponisation of space; global militarism that continues to drain desperately needed resources from programmes that enhance life; and other peace and justice issues that effect the human family.

Bernice Kring

Those of us with the time and the energy have become activists — marching; protesting; visiting our elected officials; giving speeches to motivate others to action; publishing international newsletters and other materials; and even committing acts of civil disobedience when all else fails. 'Stay at home' members help keep our work alive by writing & calling elected officials, circulating petitions, keeping us in their prayers, guiding their grandchildren in the ways of non-violence, and helping to raise funds for our Peace & Justice Scholarship Awards, plus other specific humanitarian efforts we adopt.

In most cultures around the world, grandmothers are revered as the 'keepers of the peace'. We are inspired and motivated by that fact, but realize that in today's dangerous world we can no longer keep or promote peace by sitting in our rocking chairs!

We remain an all-volunteer organization and prefer to maintain an informal structure that encourages others to start, with very little effort, chapters in their communities.

The world is a safer place 'in grandma's arms'.

CONTACT: Lorraine Krofchok
PO Box 580788
Elk Grove, CA 95758   USA
lorraine@grandmothersforpeace.org

GRANDMOTHERS FOR PEACE UK

The UK chapter is active in planning and supporting demonstrations against the curtailment of civil liberties, the proposed renewal of the Trident weapons system and the commemoration of the 25th anniversary of the Greenham Common women's peace camp.

CONTACT: Jean Stead
020 7435 8931
jeanstead@hotmail.com

TOFF

TOFF ('distinguished person, swell', OED) aptly describes just one of the many fine qualities portrayed by our numerous and varied members. Coming from all walks of life and many different ethnic groups, the only necessary qualification is to be over 50 years' young. We take them here: Moscow and St Petersburg. We take them there: Beijing, Xian and Cuba. We take them everywhere: Brussels, Strasbourg, Reims and many places in between. They are a terrific group of women – and men – who climbed the Great Wall of China, explored the Kremlin and regularly give our London Members of the European Parliament (MEPS) a good grilling. We always have a good mix of people who join in the group activities and enjoy stimulating conversations.

TOFF was started by Carlie and Stephen Newman in 2002. We organise visits to the European Parliament in either Brussels or Strasbourg, together with sight seeing, wine or champagne tasting and excursions to places of interest en route.

Literally by popular demand we have continued to organise our Eurotrip plus we have 'branched out' into other countries and areas of interest. We also took a group to a hotel in the Bay of Cadiz, Spain where we participated in adult education courses as well as enjoying excursions and very tasty food. There are plans for a trip to the American music cities – Branson, Memphis, Tennessee and Nashville – with visits to the Grand Ole Opry and, of course, Elvis Presley's Gracelands.

We go to places that we will enjoy and our experience so far, along with comments from our TOFF companions, seem to endorse our choices. We try to keep costs down while ensuring that all rooms have private facilities and we are able to undertake visits in reasonable comfort!

TOFF is a member organisation of the London Civic Forum. TOFF is a non-profit making voluntary organisation. It relies primarily on friends and colleagues passing on information to others.

CONTACT: Carlie & Stephen Newman
5 Straffan Lodge
Belsize Grove
London NW3 4XE
020 7586 6440   Mobile: 07973 932 665
Toff@toffs.org
www.toffs.org

THE THELMA AND LOUISE CLUB

Thelma & Louise club is an exclusive network for women. The club enables members to meet like-minded women, find travel buddies and plan dream adventures!

Registration to Thelma & Louise club (TLc) is free and allows women to input their profile and start looking for travel buddies. Fully-fledged membership costs £9.99 per year and for this members are able to communicate with other TLc members, use instant messaging and access the message boards.

Members can also enjoy holidays ranging from leisurely tours to challenging adventures, day trips, articles, plus TLc's favourite products and services.

CONTACT: Thelma and Louise club
10 High Street
West Molesey KT8 2NA
www.thelmandlouise.com

AGE CONCERN ENGLAND

Age Concern England has a wide range of information available covering all aspects of later life. Their website provides links to many useful sites. Free Factsheets cover a wide range of issues including pensions, health, care and leisure activities. These are available online, by email or phone the Information Line 0800 00 99 66.

CONTACT: Age Concern England
Astral House
1268 London Road
London SW16 4ER
www.ageconcern.org.uk

Ageing Well UK is a health promotion initiative that enables you to take control of your own health and promote healthy lifestyles to your peers. The programme recruits and trains volunteers who are 50 years or over to become Senior Health Mentors. Volunteers then make contact with isolated people and community groups, providing vital links to health services and opportunities in local communities.

CONTACT: aau@ace.org.uk

Opening Doors is the umbrella title of Age Concern's developing programme of publications, resources and events for and about older lesbians, gay men and bisexuals in the UK. The Age Concern website also has an extensive list of links to other organisations of interest to older lesbians.

CONTACT: Antony Smith,
National Development and Policy Officer Older Lesbians, Gay Men and Bisexuals
020 8765 7576
OpeningDoors@ACE.org.uk

SENIORS NETWORK

Seniors Network is a website which as well as offering a wide variety of information and links to sites focusing on, for instance, health, leisure and book reviews, has a particular interest in campaigns to improve the lot of pensioners and the work of the National Pensioners Convention.

CONTACT: www.seniorsnet.co.uk
John Lynch 01236 435156

HELP THE AGED

Help the Aged is an international charity fighting to free disadvantaged older people from poverty, isolation and neglect.

Help the Aged campaigns for change in government policy, undertakes research into the needs of older people and provides local services in communities across the UK and overseas.

We provide a range of services for disadvantaged older people around the UK, where our aim is to enable them to live independently in their own homes for as long as they wish.

Whether you are looking for advice on claiming benefits, or need information about home security, our range of regularly updated leaflets can help.

CONTACT: Help the Aged
207-221 Pentonville Road
London N1 9UZ
020 7278 1114
SeniorLine: 0808 800 6565
(Textphone-Minicom 0800 26 96 26)
Seniorline in Northern Ireland: 0808 808 7575

UNIVERSITY OF THE THIRD AGE

The U3A in the UK started in 1982. It was based on the belief that Third Agers had the skills to organise and teach in their own autonomous learning groups. Since U3A members learn for the pleasure of it, no qualifications are required and none are given. The subjects tackled vary with each U3A and the number  of groups offered will depend on the size and enthusiasm of the local U3A.

There are currently nearly 600 U3As in the UK with a total membership of over 150,000. The website or National Office can give you information about your nearest group. In addition, the National Development Officer or a Regional Coordinator can assist with the setting up of new U3As. Send an SAE for the address of your nearest U3A or check the website.

The national organisation also offers access to online learning opportunities, contact with national subject or activity-based networks, and travel opportunities.

CONTACT: U3A
Old Municipal Buildings
19 East Street
Bromley BR1 QH

020 8466 6139
www.u3a.org.uk
national.office@u3a.org.uk

AGE EXCHANGE

Age Exchange has, for more than 20 years, been developing new models of work offering participants a wide range of reminiscence-based creative activities and arts products. They are recognised nationally and internationally by many providers of services in the statutory and voluntary sectors as being the leading practitioners, consultants and sources of information about reminiscence work.

The Reminiscence Centre in Blackheath, south-east London, receives thousands of visitors each year. It functions as:

* a national reminiscence training and resource centre, the home of the country's leading professional reminiscence theatre company

* a museum of everyday life in the first half of the 20th century

* a flourishing hive of inter-generational and educational activities

* a local community centre with cultural and social activities

* a gallery with changing exhibitions and the headquarters of the UK and European Reminiscence Networks

Age Exchange offers training for health & social services staff, community arts workers, teachers, librarians . . . anyone interested in developing reminiscence groups.

Their publications provide a highly entertaining and educational way of exploring living memory.

CONTACT: The Reminiscence Centre
11 Blackheath Village
London SE3 9LA
020 8318 9105
administrator@age-exchange.org.uk
www.age-exchange.org.uk

OLDER AND BOLDER

OLDER AND BOLDER (NIACE - National Institute for Adult Continuing Education)

Older and Bolder aims:

- to promote wider learning opportunities for older people

- to promote and actively create learning opportunities for those older people not normally involved in any such provision

- to promote wider participation by older adults in all forms of learning

- to better understand and subsequently facilitate the learning needs of those traditionally absent from most kinds of learning

- to promote awareness of the contribution older people can and do make to learning and how that is achieved

- to recognise and promote choice of learning for older people for their own purposes: for personal interest, for work or for fun

- to promote good practice in education and training for older people, recognising the needs of carers and support workers

- to influence policy in all areas that might affect provision and participation

To attain these ends, Older & Bolder:

- runs an annual national conference

- publishes a newsletter 3 times a year

- runs the Senior Learner of the Year Award in England as part of Adult Learners' Week celebrations

- awards the Older & Bolder Institutional Awards annually to examples of outstanding and replicable good practice

- facilitates the development of local and regional collaborative working

- gathers data to further the debate and influence future educational and social policy

The NIACE/Older & Bolder website has some excellent links to other sites that will be of interest to readers.

CONTACT: Older & Bolder, NIACE
Renaissance House, 20 Princess Road West
Leicester LE1 6TP
www.niace.org.uk/Research/older_bolder   Email: jim.soulsby@niace.org.uk

OTHER THIRD AGE PRESS BOOKS

Third Age Press

. . . an independent publishing company which recognizes that the period of life after full-time employment and family responsibility can be a time of fulfilment and continuing development . . . a time of regeneration

Third Age Press books are available by direct mail order from

Third Age Press, 6 Parkside Gardens London SW19 5EY

Email: dnort@globalnet.co.uk

Website: www.thirdagepress.co.uk

All prices include UK p&p for up to 2 books.

For 3 or more books please add £1 per book.

Please add 20% for postage to other countries.

UK Sterling cheques payable to Third Age Press.

Dianne Norton ~ Managing Editor

---

www.wwwow.info

. . . is a new website launched by Third Age Press *in conjunction with the publication of* DEFINING WOMEN.

❀ *It contains links to and details of organisations of interest to older women. We hope that this list will grow as more people and organisations discover the book and the website. Please feel free to contribute information.*

❀ *Through the website readers can also express their opinions on the issues raised in* DEFINING WOMEN.

WHY WWWOW?   *Wonderful Worldly Wise Older Women?*

OUR GRANDMOTHERS
OUR MOTHERS
OURSELVES

Charmian Cannon (Editor)

Eleven women who met through a U3A group exploring
women's hidden social history talked, and then wrote,
about their grandmothers, their mothers and their own
lives. Their stories spanned the whole 20th Century,
encompassed two world wars and many social and
political changes affecting women. Through their
discussions they crossed class and ethnic boundaries
and exchanged their experiences of education, work and
home life. They shared intimate family recollections
honestly ~ uncovering affectionate as well as painful
memories.

The book includes a section on the increasing use of life histories as a way
of linking personal lives and public events, and a list of sources and further
reading.

200 pages   £9.95

CHANGES AND CHALLENGES IN LATER LIFE:
LEARNING FROM EXPERIENCE

Edited by Yvonne Craig

Foreword by Claire Rayner ~ illustrated by Maggie Guillon

*Older people share with those of all ages the desire for fulfilment - a need to transform
surviving into thriving.* This book brings together experts from Britain's major caring
organisations to share their wealth of experience and practical advice on the sometimes
difficult situations of later life. The wealth of experience concentrated in this book shows
how changes and challenges can lead to positive attitudes and action.

160 pages   £5.00

AN EXPERIMENT IN LIVING:
SHARING A HOUSE IN LATER LIFE

by June Green, Jenny Betts & Greta Wilson

Truthful, humorous, thought-provoking, considered and practical . . . this book is an introduction to a potential new lifestyle by three wise women. But the book is more than just a guide to how to set up house together. Interspersed with the practicalities the three authors have each reflected on *What's in it for them* and their individual attitudes to retirement.

The book, ***An Experiment in Living,*** is out of print. However, Third Age Press is making the full text available as an A4 transcript.

£5.00

JUST IN CASE . . .
MAKING A HOME FOR ELDERLY PEOPLE

by Pat Howard
illustrated by Maggie Guillon

For over 25 years Pat Howard was heavily involved in the welfare of older people. This is a book to . . .

• inspire and encourage anyone working with older people

• offer advice and reassurance to any one considering moving into a home or looking for a home for someone else.

196 pages £5.00

 *.. is a series that focuses on the presentation of your unique life. These booklets seek to stimulate and guide your thoughts and words in what is acknowledged to be not only a process of value to future generations but also a personally beneficial exercise.*

Four books by Eric Midwinter

A VOYAGE OF REDISCOVERY: A GUIDE TO WRITING YOUR LIFE STORY

. . . is a 'sea chart' to guide your reminiscence & provide practical advice about the business of writing or recording your story

36 pages	£4.50

ENCORE: A GUIDE TO PLANNING A CELEBRATION OF YOUR LIFE

An unusual and useful booklet that encourages you to think about the ways you would like to be remembered, hopefully in the distant future.

20 pages £2.00

THE RHUBARB PEOPLE

Eric Midwinter's own witty and poignant story of growing up in Manchester in the 1930s. Also on audio cassette including useful tips on writing or recording your story.

32 pages £4.50
~ audio cassette £5.00

GETTING TO KNOW ME

. . . is aimed at carers and families of people in care. It provides the opportunity to create a profile of an older person ~ their background and relationships, likes and dislikes, as well as record the practical information needed to make the caring process a positive experience for all concerned. The end result should be a valuable tool for any carer.

24 pages £2.00

LIFESCAPES: THE LANDSCAPES OF A LIFETIME

by Enid Irving

. . . introduces whole new art form . . . **Lifescape** is a collage of memories. Make one just for fun or as a very special family heirloom. *Lifescapes* can be made by individuals, in groups, as a family or as an intergenerational activity. The resulting *Lifescape* is not only decorative but serves to increase understanding of the whole person and stimulate memory.

24 pages £4.00

Two books by Dr H B Gibson illustrated by Rufus Segar

ON THE TIP OF YOUR TONGUE:
YOUR MEMORY IN LATER LIFE

. . . explores memory's history and examines what an 'ordinary' person can expect of their memory. He reveals the truth behind myths about memory and demonstrates how you can manage your large stock of memories and your life. Wittily illustrated by Rufus Segar.

151 pages £7.00

A LITTLE OF WHAT YOU FANCY DOES YOU GOOD:
YOUR HEALTH IN LATER LIFE

Managing an older body is like running a very old car - as the years go by you get to know its tricks and how to get the best out of it, so that you may keep it running sweetly for years and years . . . so says Dr H B Gibson in his sensible and practical book which respects your intelligence and, above all, appreciates the need to enjoy later life.

256 pages   £7.00

OR buy both books together for £10

CONSIDER THE ALTERNATIVES:
HEALTHY STRATEGIES FOR LATER LIFE

Dr Caroline Lindsay Nash   illustrated by Maggie Guillon

. . . offers a clear and unbiased explanation of the nature and uses of a wide range of alternative therapies . . . what you can expect of complementary medicine . . . and why yoga, pets, music and humour can contribute to your personal strategy for a healthy third age. Contributions from Dr Michael Lloyd, a psychologist specialising in the management of pain, and from pensioner, Tony Carter, on how and why he thinks you should take control of your own health.

160 pages £5.00

THE PLAY READER:
7 DRAMAS BY THIRDAGERS

Seven one-act plays ideal for reading in groups, rehearsed readings or performance. Their rich variety is certain to challenge and stimulate as well as provide entertainment.

Includes: a mystery set in 1900's Paris; a psychological drama; all-women play set in Roman Britain; Greek holiday setting; the Third Age of the future?; family drama; comedy duet for two women.

Now available in A4 format, hole punched (binder not included ~ may be photocopied).

126 pages   £10.00

Third Age Press is planning a second collection of plays for reading. Details will be announced on the Third Age Press website and in *U3A News*.

NO THANKS TO LLOYD GEORGE:
THE FORGOTTEN STORY - HOW THE OLD AGE PENSION WAS WON

by Dave Goodman   Foreword by Jack Jones

No Thanks to Lloyd George tells a story of passion, dedication, determination and grit. From 1898 old people, living in fear of the work house, thronged to packed meetings all over the country to hear how their lives could be transformed by the introduction of a pension. But it took more than ten years of struggle and disappointment before the first British old people collected five shillings from their post offices.

96pages   £3.50

Books by Eric Midwinter

BEST REMEMBERED ...
A HUNDRED STARS OF YESTERYEAR

... presents a galaxy of 100 stars from the days before
television ruled our lives. These cultural icons achieved
lasting fame through radio, cinema, stage, dance hall,
theatre, variety hall and sporting field between 1927 and 1953 – a quarter
century rich in talent, innovation, humour and unforgettable melodies. As a
trigger for reminiscence or a rich but light scholarly text on social and cultural
history, its lively style and fizzing illustrations cannot fail to please.

illustrated by Rufus Segar
168 pages   £10.95

THE PEOPLE'S JESTERS
TWENTIETH CENTURY BRITISH COMEDIANS

At one level, *The People's Jesters* is an absorbing exercise in nostalgia, with its
perceptive and amusing profiles of scores of well-loved and well-remembered
comics, from George Robey and Will Hay, via Max Miller and Tommy Handley,
to Tony Hancock and Morecambe and Wise. Beyond that, it is an astute and
definitive analysis of how comedians worked. With its combine of colourful
content and shrewd comment, there are rich pickings here for all manner of
readers.

SPECIAL OFFER
Buy *The People's Jesters*
together with *Best Remembered*
for the combined price of only
£20.00

Eric Midwinter's lifelong interest in
comedians began 70 years ago when he
saw Albert Modley in pantomime. He
thus brings untold memories, as well
as his noted skills as a well-known
social historian and commentator, to
the task of describing and judging
the major age of the comedians.

232 pages   £14.50

500 BEACONS: THE U3A STORY

by Eric Midwinter

The British University of the Third Age (U3A), launched in 1982, has proved to be one of the most successful exercises in social co-operation, radical adult education and older age citizenship since World War II. This is the tale of the origins, the development, the current position and the future aspirations of this unique pioneering of the principles of mutual aid. While closely analysing the national and regional elements in this dramatic success story, the book's focus is also on the many local stories of individuals battling to make the U3A ideal work amid the homes and streets of their own town or community.

The author is Dr Eric Midwinter, the distinguished social historian and social policy analyst, himself the surviving one of the three 'Founding Fathers' of U3A in the UK.

320 pages   £12.50   [U3A members £10.00]

NOVEL APPROACHES: A GUIDE TO THE POPULAR CLASSIC NOVEL

by Eric Midwinter

Oh for a good read and an un-putdownable book! Despite the lurid blandishments of television, there are still many of us who turn, quietly, pensively, to the novel in leisure moments. This short text is aimed at such people whose interest has been kindled sufficiently to permit some extra contemplation and study.

Novel Approaches takes 35 novels that have stood the test of time and embeds them in historical and literary commentary - a combination of social background giving scientific objectivity, and the author's artistic subjectivity.

180 pages   £9.50

It is sad to grow old but nice to ripen

Brigitte Bardot